RON PIGRAM

Disco
Walks in the
Chilterns

SHIRE PUBLICATIONS LTD

Contents

*The publishers thank Ginny Elsemere for revising the walks for
this third edition.*

Introduction

"Where are the Chilterns?" the author was asked in London. The question was mildly surprising, for the long dramatic chalk rises and deep vales dark-blurred with the ever-changing colour of beech-woods that stretch north and eastwards from the Thames valley are so close to London that much of the area is within an hour's ride from it. Yet it is so remote, away from the roads, that the visitor could be a hundred miles or many hours from the noise and smell of modern urban living. For many years the Chiltern Hills have been able to survive the disfigurement which other parts of the Home Counties have suffered through being close to London; its country-side is still refreshing, although slowly it is being eroded by housing and motorways. Still, the Chiltern Hills are there to be discovered and enjoyed for as long as the leisure time you have to spend. Even amongst those who know and love these hills, few know every path or byway. There is always a new discovery for walkers who probe the hills; and each new walk, however short, can be a new adventure. This book seeks to guide the explorer into the best-loved parts of the Chiltern Hills within easy reach of London. There is much, much more to see but if you follow the paths in these pages your day will be well spent; if your appetite to explore deeper into the hills is whetted you will already have fallen under the Chiltern spell — an appreciation of nature that men have known for thousands of years.

About the walks

The walks in this book are all circular, especially designed so that they can be undertaken by explorers arriving by car (you can join the guide at any point). Each walk also starts near a railway station or is easily reached by bus or coach. Most of the walks can easily be shortened as shown in the text so that there is no need to undertake more in your day than you feel able to enjoy. If walking is a new experience, try a short tour — one of the finest is the walk from Wendover which climbs to Coombe Hill — the highest point of the Chilterns; although the distance is not large, the views on a fine day are spectacular. Nearer London, there are walks around Amersham and Chesham; and for the more adventurous Bledlow Ridge, above Princes Risborough, offers a challenge (and a full day's walk). There is something in this book for everyone.

You can, if you wish, regard the instructions as a series of guidelines and clues on your day of discovery. Minor changes in the countryside, particularly in those parts of the Chilterns nearest London, are always occurring and these may give the odd moment or so of difficulty. Usually a careful study of a map will soon make it clear which direction to take. The Chiltern Society Footpath maps cover all the walks in this book. They are drawn to a scale of 2½ inches to the mile and show all public rights of way.

Every care has been taken to see that the paths are open to the public although there can be no guarantee that rights of way still exist. Parking for cars can be found near the starting points of walks. Travel details are for guidance only; check before setting out, as many buses run only on weekdays.

The Chiltern Society's volunteer field groups have waymarked many of the footpaths used in this book. The mark, a white broad arrow painted on a stile or on a tree, is a friendly sign confirming your way ahead.

The going, especially on open chalk paths, can be slippery in wet weather and mud should be anticipated near farms. Take the countryman's example and be well-shod if the weather seems to be changeable. Finally, parts of the Chilterns can be some distance from an alehouse or inn; it is often wise to take refreshments with you.

Help the farmer

There are many ways of taking care so that you help the countryman as you enjoy your day in the country. Make sure that you fasten all gates to prevent cattle from straying, and try to keep to the paths, as far as possible, across farmland. Footpaths tend to get ploughed up during the autumn — the finest season to visit the Chilterns — and, although the paths should be restored, the way may have to be redefined. Please walk in single file on field paths; it helps to make the path clear.

Please leave the wild flowers for others to enjoy. Some parts of the Chilterns visited in this book do expose reminder notices — Chinnor Hill nature reserve is a case in point — but wild flowers, especially bluebells, seldom survive the journey home. Finally, do take your litter home with you. By your consideration you will repay the local people for the pleasure the countryside has given you.

The beechwoods

The beech tree, which grows in profusion and to great heights on the steep slopes of the Chilterns, has helped to found the most important local industry of the area, furniture making. A rural craftsman, known as a bodger, worked alone under the tall trees deep in the woods among his raw material, fashioning small items of furniture from a simple lathe whose action often relied on a springy branch. These men, a fiercely independent breed, have now largely died out and although furniture making is still important in some towns, especially High Wycombe, the industry no longer relies on the locally grown beech for its supplies.

4

Travel enquiries
British Rail: 01-262 6767 or your nearest station.
Underground: 01-222 1234.
London Country Buses and Green Line Coaches: 01-834 6563 or
   Reigate 42411.
High Wycombe Bus Station Travel Office: High Wycombe (0494)
   20941.

Chiltern Society Footpath Maps

These maps are especially drawn to a scale of 24 inches to the mile, and each map covers approximately 24 square miles, with all public rights of way boldly shown and individually identified by definitive map reference number. Suggested walks in the area are described on the reverse of each map, and they are printed on a robust stock which folds down to 8 by $5\frac{1}{4}$ inches. Maps already published are:

1. Marlow and District
2. Henley Northwest
3. Wendover and District
4. Henley Southwest
5. Sarratt and Chipperfield
6. The Penn Country
7. Wycombe Northwest
8. Chartridge and Cholesbury
9. The Oxfordshire Escarpment
10. Ewelme and District
11. The Hambleden Valley
12. The Hughenden Valley
13. Beaconsfield and District
14. Stokenchurch and District
15. Crowmarsh and Nuffield
16. Goring and Mapledurham
17. Chesham and Berkhamsted
18. Tring and District
19. Ivinghoe and Ashridge

The maps are published and districted by Shire Publications Limited on behalf of the Chiltern Society. They are available from local booksellers but, if in difficulty, you can order them direct from Shire Publications Ltd., Cromwell House, Church Street, Princes Risborough, Aylesbury, Bucks. HP17 9AJ.

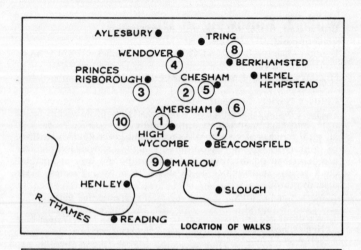

AYLESBURY ●   ●TRING
               ⑧
   WENDOVER●   ●BERKHAMSTED
           ④
PRINCES   CHESHAM   ●HEMEL
RISBOROUGH●   ② ⑤   HEMPSTEAD
    ③   ⑤
         AMERSHAM● ⑥
   ⑩   ①
     HIGH   ⑦
     WYCOMBE ●BEACONSFIELD

        ⑨●MARLOW
   HENLEY●
R. THAMES   ●SLOUGH
        ●READING
              LOCATION OF WALKS

KEY TO SKETCH MAPS

※   START OF WALK
◄━·━·━   ROUTE OF WALK
━··━··━   ALTERNATIVE ROUTE
Ⓟ   CAR PARK
═══   ROAD
::::::   TRACK
- - - - - OTHER FOOTPATHS
■   BUILDING
⊞   CHURCH
P. H.   PUBLIC HOUSE
〰〰   RIVER OR STREAM
◎   WATER FEATURE
+●+   RAILWAY AND STATION
) (BRIDGE
♠♣ ♀♂   WOODLAND

6

Walk 1. Following in Dizzy's footsteps

Circular tour from High Wycombe or West Wycombe via Downley. Common and Bradenham (10 miles).

Isaac Disraeli, the father of Benjamin Disraeli, favourite statesman of Queen Victoria, was the tenant of the manor-house at Bradenham until his death in 1848 at the age of 81. Young Benjamin grew to love the beautiful surrounding hills and woods so dearly that he knew all the paths, especially the way to his final home, Hughenden Manor, across Naphill Common. This tour from High Wycombe has to penetrate the town's housing development to reach Dizzy's home, but it explores countryside so fine that the day will be unforgettable. The walk can also be made from West Wycombe (for walkers arriving by car) and can be shortened at Downley Common by following the instructions.

The walk starts from **High Wycombe** station. (If you arrive by bus or coach, walk through the town to Frogmore, the wide area in the centre of the town.) From the station go along Castle Street, almost opposite the station, to Frogmore, then turn right in this wide street to pass under a railway bridge and along Hughenden Road. At the first turning on the left, Bellfield Road, at the mini roundabout, turn off and after 200 yards bear right (by the right-hand side of Kingdom Hall) to pass a factory and bear right uphill by a path that reaches a housing estate. Go left, steeply uphill, by this road (Hughenden Avenue), take the second road on the right and then left at the crossing road (Telford Way).

Soon, just after 144 Telford Way, you turn right beside a wooden fence to reach **Great Tinker's Wood** (National Trust). A wide path running just inside the left edge of the wood (backs of houses beyond) brings you to the end of the wood. Turn right just before this by a path that drops, just inside the wood, to the lower corner, where turn left across the field, pass the monument ahead, not forgetting to notice your first wide views over the Chilterns. The obelisk, now protected by a fence, was erected by Dizzy's wife to the memory of his father, whose house is passed later. Isaac was the author of a book called *Curiosities of Literature* — a work that the lady felt placed him among the immortals.

Beyond, the path plunges into **Little Tinker's Wood,** also owned by the National Trust. The path bears leftward and runs on generally level ground to the far side where you turn right, passing the back gardens of a few houses, to a lane at **Downley.** Go ahead by Narrow Lane (past new housing development) to a wide area of grass land — this is **Downley Common.**

Cross the road and bear half left to the rough path opposite that winds down to a track in front of the small chapel, dating from the 1840s, in a hollow on the common's far left side. (Here you may return to High Wycombe by way of Hughenden Manor if your time is limited — bear half-right across the common ahead towards the bus terminus at the end of the road and follow the instructions on page 11.)

The line of the main walk continues, from the chapel, by going right uphill towards the common ahead, then, when the track circles leftwards around some cottages, strike half-left (aiming for a public seat) to meet a lane by a small red brick shed beside a pair of bus stop posts.

Now leave the commonland behind by taking a stony track, starting only a few yards to the right of the building, that serves a cottage ahead. Go through a gateside swing-gate on the left before reaching the house through another swing-gate and follow the right side of a field to a beechwood. There are wide views towards the West Wycombe heights. The path drops down into a small valley in the wood. Here you turn left, dropping gently downhill in the wonderful cradle-track until you emerge, through a field gate, at a metalled lane. The impressive stand of beech in the distance is Great Cookshall wood.

The lane leads leftwards to a bend after 300 yards. Go *forward* as it turns away, to a stile, high on the folds of the hills. Aim for a stile at the end of the hedgeline below, cross it and another in the hedge on the far side of a farm track, and follow a right-hand hedge over the rise and down under a railway arch and then slightly left over a field to the main Wycombe-Risborough road. As you approach the railway, on the far slopes can be seen West Wycombe church surmounted by its golden ball and the Dashwood Mausoleum. From a vee-stile opposite go uphill past a converted farm on the right and go over a stile at the second field gate on the right to bring the wire field-division on your left. The path quickly reaches a small lane running around the hill on which **West Wycombe** church stands.

For the village and Hell Fire Caves, go downhill. The walk continues along the lane uphill to reach a point where the way divides — the rough track on the right leading to Windyhaugh while the lane turns leftwards to a car park, a convenient point for walkers arriving by car at West Wycombe to start the walk. It is also easy to visit the church (and admire the view) from here.

WEST WYCOMBE VILLAGE and West Wycombe Park are the property of the National Trust. The mansion, on the far side of the main road (downhill) was built in the eighteenth century for Sir Francis Dashwood. He founded the Hell Fire Club, a sort of extremist group of the day, who held meetings in the secrecy of the tunnels hewn in the chalk hill below the church.

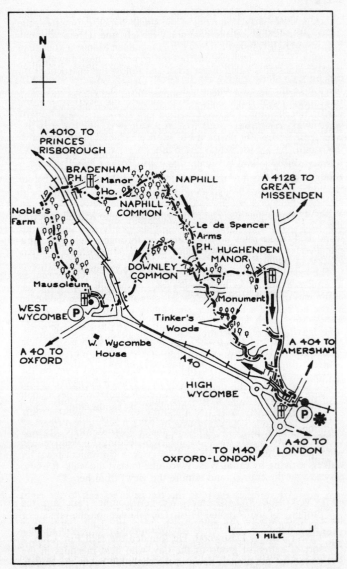

N

A 4010 TO
PRINCES
RISBOROUGH

BRADENHAM
P.H.
Manor
Ho.

NAPHILL

NAPHILL
COMMON

A 4128 TO
GREAT
MISSENDEN

Noble's
Farm

Le de Spencer
Arms
P.H. HUGHENDEN
MANOR

DOWNLEY
COMMON

Mausoleum

Monument

WEST
WYCOMBE
P

Tinker's
Woods

A 40 TO
OXFORD

W. Wycombe
House

A 40

A 404 TO
AMERSHAM

HIGH
WYCOMBE

P

TO M40
OXFORD-LONDON

A 40 TO
LONDON

1

1 MILE

9

The entrance to Hell Fire Caves, which are open to the public, is just downhill. St. Laurence's church was once the church of the lost village of Haveringdon.

To leave West Wycombe, take the very rough grassy path that can be seen starting between the posts where the lane divides at the top of the rise leading to the car park. This soon becomes a fine broad ridge track which runs on into the heart of a wonderful beechwood. For over a mile the track, a half-forgotten wagonway, continues — at first you can look out towards the west from your lofty position but soon the track buries deep into the wood. At a fork, when the fields on your right give way to trees, continue straight on by the main track. Later it passes a plantation of firs and finally reaches Nobles Farm. The way continues some twenty yards or so past it. Here leave the track at an area of hard standing and follow a faint path downhill through the woods into a field on the right.

Look for the wild flowers — moon-daisies, sage-flowers and the yellow charlock — as you keep downhill, winding round by the right side of a lower field to a stile in the hedge and on to another at the railway crossing. Beyond the tracks keep on to the main road and take the turning by the Red Lion opposite to yet another National Trust property — the spacious green of **Bradenham** with its church and Manor House (the one tenanted by the Disraelis) on the far side.

BRADENHAM has a stately seventeenth-century manor house which is now used as a training college. The fine wrought-iron gates are also of this period. St. Botolph's church was heavily restored in 1865, but the south doorway is Norman. The most interesting part is the side (Windsor) chapel; notice the fine monument to Elizabeth West (1713). The figures of the man and girl support the pediment with boredom as though aware of their eternal task. Below the chapel floor is a vault which was permanently closed at the time of the 1865 restoration. When the vault was examined in 1962 it was damp-free and the twenty coffins, of cedar and lead with an elm covering, had not disintegrated. The parents of Disraeli lie within this vault.

A gravel track that starts at the top of the green to the right of the Manor House runs uphill beside the wall of the mansion to a corner where the way splits. Take the right-hand track running steeply uphill. After passing another lattice-windowed cottage and its garden go forward by a broad grassy path as the gravel track turns sharply right, at the fringe of **Naphill Common** (shown as 'Napple' on old maps), and keep forward for 60 yards or so until the path forks. There are many ways across the common from here; the left-hand fork will bring you out (following electricity cables) to the north side of the common. The route of the walk, however, is by the *right*-hand fork and is waymarked as a bridle path. The broad track splits in 200 yards. Ignore the path running away to the right and let the main path take you onward through the deep glades. Later the path crosses another in a valley in the wood and at the next main track division bear on by the right-hand (clearer) track. Soon you will be confronted with a choice of three tracks ahead. Ignore the track on the right which runs near the edge of the wood, and keep ahead by the central broad track until it spills out into an area of open fern ahead — the far side of the common.

Modern houses can be seen on the left and then you will glimpse a cottage or two. Upon reaching a broad grassy border track near the fronts of the houses, turn right and continue forward to a car turning area, and a metalled lane. Keeping your direction, continue by the lane with the common on your right until the metalling ends at posts. For another 250 yards the path continues (with the hedge left) until it breaks leftwards to another car turning point.

Here you will see iron and wooden posts ahead and a choice of two ways. Take the left path to enter, between posts, a path through **Box Wood.** Keep ahead near the right side of the wood for 100 yards or so, and upon approaching some deep, well-trodden ravines inside the wood, bear slightly left, choosing a ridge path that will keep the depressions generally on your left. In 150 yards you should see on the left a cottage, the first of a row. Leave the wood between some more iron posts and carry on along a rough track passing the row of cottages and the small Le De Spenser Arms public house. (Note, if you reach only a *solitary* cottage on passing through the wood you should turn leftwards until you see the row of cottages.) The track runs on to the start of the metalled road at **Downley Common.**

(Walkers who are turning for West Wycombe should follow the road to the far side of the common, picking up instructions at page 8.)

For the return to High Wycombe, keep forward by the rough track at the bus turn, passing some more cottages on your left. Soon the track turns sharply left towards a yellow cottage. At this turn continue *ahead* for 30 yards or so over the grass to reach a clear track that runs downhill between the banks of fern ahead, lining the east side of the common. Ignore the left-hand path just inside the wood and descend to a hollow and intersection of paths (oddly this little dell has its own fire hydrant). Take the left-hand track (passing the yellow H on the tree just to your left) and go down a falling path between groves of young trees to reach a field, then on by the clear

11

enclosed path that leads over it, through a wood, and up to **Hughenden Manor,** where turn left along the drive.

HUGHENDEN MANOR was purchased by Disraeli in 1848. It is now open to the public as the Disraeli Museum and is a National Trust house. The lovely parkland here is owned by the Trust and also by the High Wycombe Council. Queen Victoria was so fond of her prime minister that she ordered her carriage to follow the route taken by Disraeli on his last visit to Windsor Castle, when she visited Hughenden after his death.

Beyond the cattle grid and gates, turn right over the parkland, gradually descending the slope to pass through an iron wicket gate by a Scots pine. Then pass under trees to make for the stream and a stile in the fence by it. Continue through the park with the stream on your left until you reach a by-road. Turn left to the main road and **High Wycombe** is to your right. A short cut to the station is by way of Priory Avenue, on the left.

Getting there
High Wycombe: British Rail from Marylebone.
    Green Line/Oxford South Midland coaches 290, 291, 790 from London (Victoria) and Uxbridge; 290, 790 from Oxford.
    London Country buses from: Chesham, Amersham (362); Gerrards Cross, Uxbridge (305); Staines, Windsor, Slough (441). Alder Valley buses from: Windsor, Maidenhead (315, 317, 320); Reading, Henley (328, 329); Aylesbury (323, 324).
West Wycombe: Green Line/Oxford South Midland coach 290, London-Uxbridge-High Wycombe-Oxford. Alder Valley buses 321, 332 from High Wycombe.
Downley: Alder Valley buses 310, 311 from High Wycombe.
, *Car parking:* High Wycombe station, and around the town; West Wycombe (upper car park near church); Bradenham and Naphill.

Walk 2. The Hampden country

Circular tour from Great Missenden via Prestwood, Great Hampden and Little Hampden (11 miles).

The countryside around Great Hampden church has long been of interest as the district where John Hampden, soldier-hero and militant of the Puritan cause in the seventeenth century, lived and was buried. This walk that rises and falls over the beechwoods and 'bottoms' (a Chiltern term for the vales) will take you to visit Great Hampden church where the body of Hampden was brought after his fatal wound at Chalgrove Field. In the words of Macaulay, in whose age Hampden, Cromwell and the whole of the seventeenth century revolutionary movement found especial sympathies:

'His [Hampden's] soldiers, bareheaded, escorted his body to the grave, singing as they marched, that lofty and melancholy psalm ...'

From **Great Missenden** station, turn left over the bridge and left again along a rough lane running beside the railway. (If you have come by car there is ample parking here or in the town. Alder Valley bus 345 runs from the station to Prestwood and High Wycombe, and you can take this bus to Prestwood, shortening the walk as instructed on page 17.)

The track passes houses on the right; upon reaching a side track on the right in ¼ mile, turn along it (passing a cemetery) and go uphill towards **Angling Spring Wood** — the mass of beeches you can see ahead. Just inside the wood turn leftwards, climbing the steep slope by a path that emerges to meet a rough lane at a farm.

Turn sharp right along this lane which at once becomes a track between hedges (ignore stile on right) then drops through a wood to a hollow. As the track turns left, cross a stile on the right and continue by the woodland path that strays never far from the edge of the wood. From the stile on the far side of the wood, continue by the path running half-left over a field to a little track and so to a road. About 35 yards along on the right you will discover a footpath running beside a wide track (called Church Path). The path leads through **Peterley Wood** ahead, then runs on along the side of another wood to a road (avoid all the left turns in the wood). Here turn right to a footpath that starts on the far side of the church buildings ahead. There is a bus stop (A.V. 345) nearby. Keep straight on by the hedged path which soon crosses a hollow and runs near the right side of another lovely beechwood to emerge at a gap overlooking a wide field which gives wonderful views to the south over the Hughenden valley. Carry straight forward over the field to the wood ahead, enter the wood and at once bear half-right on a falling path that soon meets a clear track running very steeply down to a field and lane below.

13

Turn right along this little backwater, screened by high hedges, for almost half a mile (past a farm entrance) until you find a stile in a hedge-gap on the right (almost opposite a similar one on the far side). Cross the stile and strike forward over the steeply rising grassy slope to the wood ahead, aiming for a point where the trees recede slightly. In the corner of the wood you will find a stile from which a path plunges ahead through the beeches of this wood (**Nanfan** or **Great Wood**). The path meets a cart-track coming in from the left. Ignore the cart-track and keep on across it. The path runs to a stile in a field. Cross into the meadow; do *not* go over another stile a few yards ahead — this is where short-distance walkers from Prestwood join the walk.

In the field, follow the hedgeline on the right to the far end, then continue forward by a line of oaks and beeches and over a double stile and ahead over grass to a stile at a lane. Here turn right to cross-roads and take the left turn (to Hampden).

A firm track on the left, after 200 yards, leads through a metal gate towards **Nanfan Farm.** When the firm track turns towards the farmhouse keep generally ahead, by a path that runs just to the left of stout timber fencing to a stile ahead. From here a faint grassy path plunges down towards the line of the fence on the far side of a dip, then on, with the fence on the left, to a stile overlooking a broad sloping field. The path passes to the left of a small copse ahead, and runs around the trees before plunging half-right to meet a sunken lane at a stile from which it is a jump down to the lane.

About 25 yards to the right there is a small gap in the beech hedge (signposted across the road). Go through to a path that runs half-right uphill through the trees to strike a drive that twists uphill. As it turns leftwards at the top of the rise towards The Old Rectory leave it to go forward into the field ahead, but at once turn left (to keep a hedge between your path and the imposing house). On the far side continue on by the drive until it reaches the open land of **Hampden Common** at a charming thatched cottage that could have come straight from a fairy-tale.

Now go right, then left at a fork to pass a school and on up the Great Hampden road at the crossway. After 150 yards or so you can enter Hampden Common (on your left) by taking the path opposite an attractive cottage. The path enters the fern and trees, quickly passing through a wire fence. Turn right and trace out a winding woodland path — always keeping the fence to your right — until it turns to a stile at the village green. Make your way to the cross-roads and the Hampden Arms, an alehouse on the corner.

Now take the surfaced lane almost facing the inn (marked 'Private — no through road'). In 100 yards or so, as it turns near cottages, you will see a footpath sign marking a grassy way beside the end house. This leads straight ahead over fields (and a metalled field track) to **Great Hampden** church.

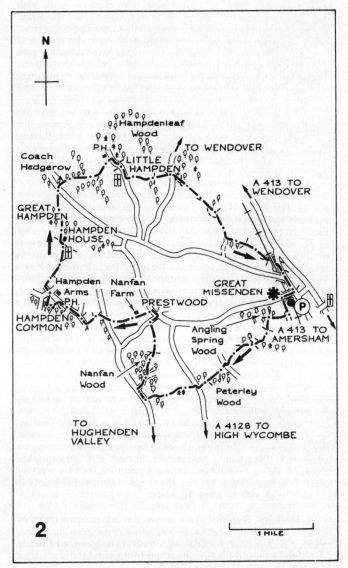

N

Hampdenleaf
Wood
P.H.
Coach
Hedgerow
LITTLE
HAMPDEN
TO WENDOVER
GREAT
HAMPDEN
A 413 TO
WENDOVER
HAMPDEN
HOUSE
Hampden
Arms
P.H.
Nanfan
Farm
GREAT
MISSENDEN
P
HAMPDEN
COMMON
PRESTWOOD
A 413 TO
AMERSHAM
Angling
Spring
Wood
Nanfan
Wood
Peterley
Wood
TO
HUGHENDEN
VALLEY
A 4128 TO
HIGH WYCOMBE

2

1 MILE

15

GREAT HAMPDEN. The fine church here is forever associated with John Hampden and the Hampden family, and it is sad that under the present arrangements here, entrance into the church at times other than for services, is prohibited, the key being tightly guarded at the Rectory, near the Hampden Arms. This is a pity, for devotees of John Hampden will admire the striking marble Hampden Monument in the chancel and a tablet to Hampden's first wife, with an epitaph by Hampden. John Hampden was lord of the manor here. The church has interesting funeral hatchments, boards or canvasses painted with the coat of arms of a dead person and carried at the funeral procession, high up in the south corner. The hatchment of the 6th Earl, Augustus Edward Hobart-Hampden, is especially interesting, for it shows in heraldic terms that when he died in 1885 he was twice married, and that he had outlived both his wives.

Turn left on the far side of the churchyard towards the stable block of **Hampden House.** The embattled mansion has almost completely swallowed the old house that Hampden knew.

Go through the white gate beyond the stables, turn right at once through another gate into a field, and go down past the tennis courts, through an area of Christmas trees, down a slope to an ancient gate in the far hedge. Here the path drops through a wood to reach a wide field, with the heights of Little Hampden Common on the far side of a shallow valley. The path runs down to the road; cross to wander uphill again by a small woodland path that leads from the stile opposite through a long, narrow belt of trees known, charmingly, as **Coach Hedgerow.** Just before the path turns left take a small path on the right which breaks through a thin screen of bushes on the right to a stile. The field here rises formidably; your path is slightly right towards a stile which can be found in the hedge on the far side. *(Note: If ground conditions are bad, it is possible to reach Little Hampden from the area of common ahead. 200 yards inside you glimpse an overgrown pit on the right. A path runs to the right uphill past the pit on the left to reach a field; then keep uphill beside hedges to Little Hampden Common, turning right past the Rising Sun to the church from where you can follow the main walk.)* After reaching the stile in the upper hedge, you continue through a plantation keeping your direction, pass through a hedge gap into a large field. Cross the field and the path continues past a cottage on the left to a rough road. Go straight ahead down the hill for a half mile to the church at **Little Hampden.**

LITTLE HAMPDEN. The quiet tiny church has occasional services but is normally kept locked; inquire nearby for the key. The row of ancient wall-paintings inside can, however, be glimpsed from its windows. Notice the unusual half-timbered porch.

For the return to Great Missenden, take the signposted footpath opposite the church — a wide grassy way that winds down, bears right around the side of a large field and heads towards the trees of **Hampdenleaf Wood** ahead, another wonderful wood that has been marred by felling in recent years. Enter the wood and bear left by the path ascending to the first beeches and go along a path that runs uphill between wire fences. The path crosses another near the top and runs on to a gap in the fence by a small field. Cross the field between wire fences to the gate, then along a drive (farm right) to a small hamlet **(Cobblers Hill)**.

Now go over the metalled lane to a track starting just left of the post box. This is the start of Mapridge Green Lane — one of a number of ancient green lanes or country trackways that once linked rural districts. The path, which can be muddy if much rain has fallen, carries straight on (ignore a footpath sign on the left); at first it meets a drive and goes ahead as a wide track, later it passes along the fringes of a wood, bears right (ignore a forward track at an obvious fork) and on gently falling ground, with wide views beyond the hedge over the Misbourne valley, runs on to reach the side of **Coneybank Wood** (left). Just at the trees there is a surprise view through the hedge gap, right, over Hampden Bottom, with the woods of Hampden Park to the right.

Only 30 yards or so after reaching the trees, leave the lane for a clear footpath on the left that plunges through the wood. The path soon runs clearly through the length of the wood before turning into a field on the left. Forward now, downwards, following the hedge on the right round the treeline and right again to a field corner. Continue down along the hedge to a gap, right, near the lower corner, drop through it (take care if the ground is wet!) into a field. The path runs clearly slantwise over the field to a stile, continues under a cattle-creep (brick arch) then bears right beyond the railway to a gate by houses on the road. **Great Missenden** town and station lie about a quarter of a mile to the right.

GREAT MISSENDEN, now freed from through traffic, is linked with its church by a bridge over the by-pass. The church's Norman font is one of its attractive features; the building was restored as late as 1900. There are many well-preserved houses along the village street representing almost every architectural period. The George is a sixteenth century coaching inn.

To shorten the walk by taking the local bus to Prestwood, leave the vehicle at the first stop after the turn at The Chequers. From a signposted gravel track on the far side of the road, a footpath leads through a small copse and along the side of a field, bearing half-right over a second field to reach the stile on page 14, line 11.

Getting there

Great Missenden: British Rail from Marylebone.
   Underground from Baker Street (change to B.R. at Amersham).
   London Country bus 359 from Amersham and Chesham.
   Bee Line bus 345 to and from High Wycombe. (Buses leave from Great Missenden station yard via Prestwood.)

Car parking: Great Missenden and en route.

Walk 3. The great escarpment

Circular walk from Princes Risborough by way of Horsenden, Bledlow Ridge, Crowell Woods and Chinnor Hill (12½ miles).

Chinnor Hill forms part of a high chalk ridge overlooking the ancient Icknield Way and the Thames Valley. The scarp slope, one of the most distant Chiltern heights, is the climax of this tour of open downland and woods that will also include a visit to the wonderful old church at Radnage. Expect some of the footpaths to be remote; there are inns on the way. This is a whole day tour; take a bus to Bledlow Ridge village if you have only an afternoon to spare.

PRINCES RISBOROUGH lies in the valley, overshadowed by some of the most striking and important Chiltern heights. The manor was known in the fourteenth century as Great Risborough. The High Wycombe-Aylesbury road winds through the attractive little town, passing its tiny Market Square and Market Hall, built in 1824. Although few of its houses are of special interest, they are old enough to give an impressive charm. St. Mary's church was completely restored in 1867. From a nearby height, the chalk clearing of Whiteleaf Cross overlooks the town.

From **Princes Risborough** station forecourt, turn left and right to the road. (Motorists will find ample parking at the station, or in the town.) Turn left along the road to pass under two railway bridges, and take a drive on the left (marked to Forest Research Laboratory) to go under a third bridge. Keep straight on when the road ends, cross a stile and follow the path to reach **Horsenden** at a charming thatched cottage. (As you reach the cottage, look for the wooden dovecote above the farm buildings.)

HORSENDEN consists of little more than St. Michael's church, the Manor House, and a cottage or two, but is a delight to visit. The dovecote, now bearing obvious signs of age, has nesting places on the upper storey, the ground floor being supported on wooden posts so that it can be used for stabling. On the far side of the lane is white-fronted Horsenden House, a mansion with charming bow windows that indicate its age as early nineteenth century. Your return path will lead you past the church; it is in fact only the chancel of a bigger building whose nave was demolished in 1765, the stones being used to build the tower. Because of this history, it has only one door, facing west. The church is usually locked; key can be found at Glebe Cottage, along the lane.

Cross to the stile opposite and keep near the right side of the fields ahead, crossing stiles to reach an iron swing-gate in the far right corner of the parkland. The path goes ahead along a drive (house right) to reach a gate and a road at **Saunderton.**

SAUNDERTON has a railway station, but it is over three miles away! It is little more than a group of cottages but in a field near the railway a Roman villa was discovered and excavated in the 1930s, although nothing can now be seen.

A footpath directly opposite leads quickly to a field; keep around its right side as it curves to cross the railway at steps. On the far side still keep near the right hedgeline; soon the path turns right to run parallel with another railway bank. Aim just left of the house ahead and you will reach a lane at a gap in the hedge. Cross to walk up the drive of the Old Rectory opposite. The drive passes to the right of the house and, as it bears sharply leftwards, the footpath runs forward to cross a stile into a field. Keep generally ahead (roughly along the ridge of the small rise in front of you) and after 250 yards or so cross a stile in the railway bank on your right, in a hollow. Beyond the single line and the far stile, bear leftwards by the path running up beside a hedge on your left. As the ground rises there are wide views towards Bledlow Ridge. At the top corner take some care (you should find a white waymark arrow on a wooden gatepost to indicate that the way is forward, shortly bearing right). You are on the Ridgeway Path here. Go on half-left to a stile near the support stays of an electricity post. Cross the stile; you are in a wide field. The next objective is the house that you see 400 yards away. Pass to the left of the hose to reach a rough drive that emerges at a metalled lane.

The bridleway opposite now leads uphill towards **Lodge Hill.** The path is clear and follows a left-hand hedge that bends first left then right. At the top corner the path runs uphill before turning leftwards around the lower slopes of the hill. (The Ridgeway Path continues on up and over the summit.)

Here you are about 630 feet up, with impressive Chiltern views. Let the track take you round to a broken gate. From here the path runs down to a valley and turns left (ignore a gate ahead) to keep on lower ground to pass **Lodge Hill Farm** (right).

(Diversion. At the farm you can shorten your walk if you do not object to rough going (see the route map). A short drive runs towards the farm to pass the buildings on your right. At a field gap 50 yards to the left, turn into a rising field and follow the right hedge to a hollow; bear left uphill to a rough lane at a house. The lane runs into the main road at Bledlow Ridge. From here you can pick up the main walk at Radnage church — go down the field path starting 30 yards to the right along the main road and after

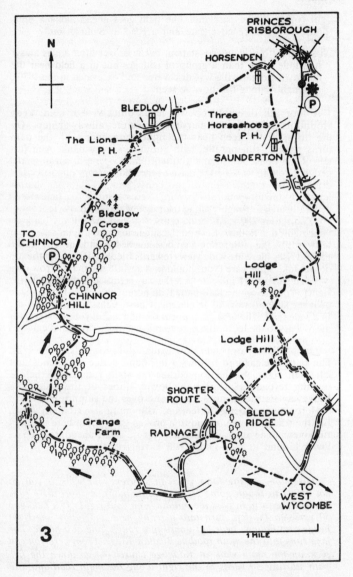

crossing a corner stile you will emerge at a height overlooking Radnage church which can just be seen in the trees below. An unofficial path winds leftward downhill to reach a point on the main walk; the official footpath is straight downhill to the lane near the church.)

The main walk continues ahead by a metalled track that starts from the farm. In three-quarters of a mile this reaches a road where you turn right, uphill, for half a mile to the main West Wycombe-Chinnor road at **Bledlow Ridge** village. (There are buses here for those who prefer a shorter distance.)

BLEDLOW RIDGE, a straggling ribbon development, runs along the long ridge of the hills, about three miles from old Bledlow village.

From the crossroads, turn left for a few yards to a signposted bridleway on the right. Beyond a house the track dwindles to a clear path plunging downwards. Do not get carried away by the urge to go down the hill, for you must look for a footpath on the right starting from an odd iron ladder stile. (It is near the top of the slope.)

Cross the stile (or go round it) and go slantwise downhill to follow the line of a hedge. Cross another stile and after 25 yards or so, follow the path into a field on the left. Climb with the path through another gap straight ahead into a second field and carry on, with the hedgeline on your right, along the upper slopes of fields, enjoying the views across the valley towards the opposite heights (Radnage Common). Ignore any paths suggesting you climb upwards and continue by the field path around the folds of the hill, with trees right, until you reach a wide grassy field as the woods end. (You are now near the diversion short-cut, not far from Radnage church.)

Strike across the grass towards the line of the hedge ahead, aiming for a point some 50 yards to the left of where the bushes abruptly end. Here you will find a stile; cross it, go slightly left to some lovely stone steps in **Radnage** churchyard wall, and walk to the church gates

RADNAGE. The thick walls of the small church here, at the intersection of many paths, gives a refreshing coolness to its interior on a hot day. Its imposing grey thirteenth century tower can be seen peeping above the surrounding trees from some distance away.

The wall-painting remains are of great interest. Much of Exodus XX stands magnified on the north wall like some enormous exposure from a film projector, and beyond the lower part of the tower (its bell-pulls are in full view of the congregation) parts of other paintings including Christ in Majesty and St.

Christopher remain to give colour to the splays of the lancet windows.

Radnage is really a collection of cottages, widely separated — some are over a mile away from the church. These isolated groups, often forming the pattern of a Buckinghamshire village, were known as 'endships' — the word 'end' appearing as part of the name.

Notice the rather fine topiary pyramid. From the church keep ahead for a few yards to a little lane, then take the footpath directly opposite to reach another lane at an iron gate. Here you turn left, then first right along a charming little backwater called Horseshoe Road. In 500 yards the way dips to pass the Three Horseshoes inn. Keep on down to a white house where the road bends at the valley floor. A fine new house dominates the junction.

The walk continues with a sharp *right* turn at the road bend along a metalled track marked 'No Through Road' (Grange Farm Road). The track heads towards the Telecom tower in the distance; it winds right after a time, later loses its surface and finally enters a wood by a cottage. Follow the waymarked path through the wood, keeping close to the right-hand edge. The path is clear and you are free to enjoy the quiet peace of this wonderful beechwood, each tree reaching to a great height in its search for light. The shade where the trees are mature is so intense that no plants can grow beneath them. For a mile you follow the woodland path; as it reaches higher ground the path becomes wider and, upon joining another bridleway coming from the left, your path becomes a deep track and turns slightly right. (You can usually find a side path here if the ground is heavy.) You are now in Oxfordshire. Finally you will emerge at a small road where you turn right for 200 yards or so to an abandoned corrugated-iron mission-hall. Just beyond take a signposted broad track leading towards a house (and poultry farm). Keep the trees ahead on your right and pass various farm shelters to the wood ahead, continuing with wire and a field on your left to a small valley ahead.

Here another path joins from the right. The way is straight ahead now through another lovely beechwood. You will find the path later moves to the right side of the wood and finally runs out, with a strand of wire on your left, to another road near **Chinnor Hill**. Turn left along the road for a quarter mile, turning right along Hill Top Lane as the road winds leftwards, and carry on along the rough lane past several houses to a car park.

CHINNOR HILL nature reserve was purchased in 1964 by the Berkshire, Buckinghamshire and Oxfordshire Naturalists' Trust. The 65 acres of chalk downland comprise of scrub, woodlands, and chalk grassland, and the Trust plan to preserve about equal areas of each so that the wild flowers, insects, trees and animals that favour each type of environment can be preserved and studied. The Trust issues a very attractive leaflet to illustrate the nature trail that runs down the chalk scarp and along the line of the prehistoric Icknield Way.

From the car park a gravel path leads into the wood, full of a variety of trees including oak, cherry, sycamore and ash. The path turns leftwards at the end of the wood into the open downland. Ignore the stiles but turn right, downhill for the climax of the day's walking — a panorama that takes in the roofs of Chinnor below to the Cotswolds Hills in the far distance. As the path continues downhill it is interesting to remember that these slopes have been walked by man for thousands of years — the Icknield Way below is part of an ancient track that reaches into Norfolk. Burial chambers excavated here have shown that Saxon warriors were laid to rest nearby. On the heights of Wain Hill is Bledlow Cross, cut into the chalk.

Further on you will pass deep chalk pits and soon a narrow sunken chalk path drops sharply down until you reach a house at a track intersection. Here you avoid the tracks on the left and pass the front of the house to a drive that starts from a barred gate. This flinty drive runs further downhill, but as it turns slightly right, keep ahead by a clear field path that runs towards the red roof of the Lions public house at **Bledlow** (most locals seem to know it as the Red Lion — perhaps a more homely name).

BLEDLOW, another beautiful Buckinghamshire village, has only one main street, shaded by elms. Around rise the heights of Wain Hill, but the cottages on the north side of the road near the church are red-brick and mellowed. The church stands by a depression known as the Lyde, now a delightful garden. There is a local rhyme which forecasts:

'They who live and do abide
Shall see the church fall into the Lyde.'

Keep ahead along the village street, past the church (notice the odd off-set clock and the lines on the tower that suggest that the clerestory was, at one time, gabled) to another road where you turn left. 100 yards downhill you will see a track on the right by a green cottage. You are now on the final section of the walk; keep forward past a wooden bungalow into a field ahead and follow its right side to a corner stile. Cross and carry on to another corner stile. The white clearing on the scarp in the distance is Whiteleaf Cross. Cross the stile, follow a narrow path left through a belt of scrub, right into a field, and on, with the hedge on your left this time, to a stile that admits you into a field through which pylons are erected. The clear track goes quite straight now to another stile and over a little brook and then over grass to reach **Horsenden** again near the church. Now turn right past the church to the small thatched cottage you met before, and bear leftwards along your outward path to **Princes Risborough** again.

Getting there
Princes Risborough: British Rail from Marylebone.
Bee Line buses 323, 324, High Wycombe-Aylesbury.
Bledlow Ridge: Alder Valley bus 332, High Wycombe-Chinnor-Thame.
Car parking: Princes Risborough, Chinnor Hill nature reserve and en route.

Walk 4. A visit to Chequers

Circular tour from Wendover by way of Coombe Hill, Whiteleaf Cross, Chequers estate and Dunsmore (12 miles, 7 miles or 5½ miles).

The Prime Minister's country house at Chequers Court, deep in the finest part of the Buckinghamshire Chilterns, is the focal point of this walk, designed in a series of loops to allow you to stroll for as long as you wish. The shortest tour will show you the visual spectacular from the highest point of the Chilterns, Coombe Hill.

WENDOVER'S position was described by Leland in his *Itinerary* of c.1540: 'The Townlet selfe of Wendover, standeth partly upon the North-East Cliffs of Chiltern Hilles'. There is much of interest in the older parts of the village, with some very charming cottages near the railway station. The church is some way from the village centre.

Turn right from the station and right along the main road for about 400 yards. As the road bears right, take the chalky track ahead that forks left through a thicket. Avoid a grassy fork on the left and keep straight ahead uphill. Soon the path spreads over a turfed slope, then runs as a stony path upward still through a gate and so to the top of **Coombe Hill.**

At the top of Coombe Hill you are 850 feet high, and on a clear day you can see far over the Vale of Aylesbury. The Boer War monument was struck by lightning in 1938 and reduced to a pile of ruined stones. It was rebuilt after the war. The prospect to the west takes in the high green rise of Beacon Hill (700 feet), passed later on this walk. To the east lie the wooded slopes of Boddington Hill — a conifer-clad height, once a beechwood that was felled by German prisoners of war in the First World War. The view you see has long been loved; here is Robert Louis Stevenson describing it in 1875 (*An Autumn Effect*): 'The great plain stretched away to the northward, variegated near at hand with the quaint pattern of the fields, but growing ever more and more indistinct until it became a hurly-burly of trees ... and snatches of slanting road'.

(From the monument, short distance walkers can return to Wendover as follows: turn leftwards, keep to the edge of the scarp to a gate in a wire fence. Turn left up the hill a short distance, with the fence on your right, to a stile in it, cross and go on by the track that runs through beeches to a lane where you turn steeply

downhill. Leave the lane and turn left just before the house at the bottom cross-road, to go along the right-hand woodland track that runs for a half mile just inside the trees. When a main cross track is met, turn left, and follow the instructions from page 30.)

The main walk continues with a left turn at the Monument, with the valley on the right. Follow the edge of the scarp to a gate at a wire fence. Turn downhill, with the wire on your left, to a broad crossing track at the bottom. Go through the gate ahead to a path which leads shortly to a road. Turn right for 100 yards and take the clear track over the field on the left — a very big one! Turn right at a track to **Ellesborough** church, standing like a fortress on a high knoll. It is a fifteenth century church with a fine monument to Lady Bridge Croke, heiress of the Hawtreys of Chequers in past times.

Leave Ellesborough (locally Ellsboro') by a stile on the left, on the far side of the cottage at the arrival track. The path runs clear half-right over a field, through a hedge and over a stile at the lower slopes of **Beacon Hill.** Go for only a few yards right to pick up the faint wide grassy path that runs upwards, generally following the lower slopes of the hill, and then winding round to a stile on the far side of the grassland at a deep box-grove. All around come wonderful views; to the right is Cymbeline's Castle, an ancient defence work. Now the path crosses the ravine by a series of steps, runs across a field and follows a rough track through trees to cross the drive of Chequers Court. Cross to the stile beside the white gate opposite.

Short-distance walkers can return to Wendover by the path round the left side of the field, skirting the trees of Whorley Wood to a stile (where there is a footpath sign). They should then follow the path beyond the stile. Keep to the path that runs round the right side of the field, through an iron gate and follow the path as it turns left and crosses the main drive of Chequers. The path continues across a field to the road bend by cottages and crosses the fence by quaint iron steps. Take the wide track to the left of the cottages to a cross track at the edge of a large beechwood. Here you meet the other short distance 'loop' walkers and should follow the instructions from page 30.

The main walk continues from the white gate along the right side of the field, using a path that climbs to a grassy ridge overlooking **Great Kimble Warren** or the Happy Valley, as it has become known to generations of walkers. Keep left (still with the field on the left) to a stile at an iron gate. Now go right, by the path from the stile, that drops pleasantly to pass the head of the deep ravine flecked with small colourful bushes and trees that provide an impressive autumn effect. Keep forward by the path that keeps gradually upwards, crosses a ditch and continues to a stile at a wide enclosed track. At this point, to which you will return after visiting Whiteleaf Cross, turn downhill for 25 yards or so and leave the track for a falling path on the left that runs to a stile. This area was once a rifle range and you will see the old grassy butts to your left. Continue by the obvious track that drops after a time, crosses a track and after 500 yards or so runs up to reach a road. Here you turn left for a small footpath that starts beside a barn near the Plough inn, some 200 yards directly ahead. This is **Lower Cadsden.** This footpath moves under trees, climbing to emerge at a golf course. Look for the iron swing-gate in the hedge ahead and, taking care to watch for flying balls, cross and pass through it and past the front of a cricket pavilion to a drive. Follow this left past the car park to the foot of Whiteleaf Hill. As the drive turns keep ahead to the start of a path, left of the gate, that winds leftwards up the steep slopes to the wide grassy area at the top.

WHITELEAF CROSS. where you now stand, gives views from almost 750 feet over the Midland plain, and the roofs of Princes Risborough a little to the left. Beyond is the escarpment at Bledlow which you can visit on Walk 3 in this book. A few yards below you is the top of the cross, gouged into the chalk. It was long considered to be Anglo-Saxon in origin but modern historical opinion points to a much later date.

The way back to Wendover starts from the path that you will see just to the left of the central group of trees at the summit. This path soon runs through new wooden fencing formed of split stakes and goes clearly downhill — at first over grass dotted with trees and later curving, as a falling woodland track, to a stile where you go forward for a few yards to the Plough inn again. Now take a track (just beyond the car park ahead) that starts from a wooden gate (beside an iron fieldgate) on the right. The grassy path, laced with stones, runs forward into a remote little vale. This track splits after 200 yards or so — keep forward (left-hand branch) with netting on the right, then wire fencing on the left. Later the track turns right and climbs hard (still with the fencing left). Finally it runs on to strike a clear bridleway at right angles. Now turn left (the deep hollow you see in the wood on your left is called **Old Killington**) and follow out to a road where you cross to a stile (and sign) on the far side of the road, about 30 yards to the right.

From the stile, a thin footpath climbs forward through the young trees of a plantation, over a fire-break clearing and on ahead through bracken and ground-growth. Beyond a line of tall trees and a crossing track, the tiny path weaves through a fir plantation to reach a stile in a wire fence. Beyond it take the right-hand one of two tracks, through a glade of ash and beech until it meets a clear track (at right angles) that has also climbed from the road. Here you turn left and follow it out of the wood and on until at last it breaks out high on the northern slopes of the hills and runs down to reach the stile on the right, shaded by the spreading boughs of a great tree, that you crossed earlier. (On the way downhill you have views, right, over Happy Valley and Beacon Hill.)

At this point, cross the stile and retrace your steps going half-right at first to breast the rise just ahead, and along the ravine head to the iron gate and stile, then half-right across a field to the stile at **Chequers** where the main walk joins the short diversion mentioned earlier. Cross this stile beside a field gate, and follow the path that runs along the right side of the vast field, beside beechwoods on the right, to an iron gate at a track. Away to the left, as you go, you will see the red-brick mansion of Chequers Court.

CHEQUERS, seen on the left, is an Elizabethan country house which, as the residence of the Prime Minister of the day, is not open to the public.The footpath crossing the drive was diverted in 1972. The house contains a fine collection of Cromwellian portraits. It was built about 1565 for the Hawtrey family; Lord Lee carefully restored it before giving the house to the nation in 1917 in order to provide the Prime Minister with a restful alternative home to Downing Street. It has often been used for important conferences; in 1971 for example the tripartite talks on Northern Ireland were held here. The name is said to derive from an owner of the estate who was connected with the Exchequer, so it is doubly apt.

From the gate continue down the track, turning left to cross the main drive of Chequers. The path continues across a field towards white cottages at **Buckmoorend.** Cross by the stile and take the track that starts just to the left of the cottages and runs up to a crossing track at the fringe of **Goodmerhill Wood** (which seems to be known locally as Chequers Wood). *Here you join the short-distance walkers.*

Continue straight over the crossing track, climbing uphill by a clear woodland path. Ignore a left turn, the Ridgeway Path, after which your path becomes less clear. After reaching the top of the hill it runs to the right of a large cleared area and then, joined by a bridleway from the left, it runs clearly forward through beeches again, along a dip, emerging at a cottage at a hedged track, which soon brings you to riding stables and a cross-track. From the stile ahead, go uphill by way of stiles, over the steep grassy rise, bearing half-left to strike a hill-top lane at a stile near **Dunsmore,** one of the highest villages in the Chilterns. Go right, passing the duck-pond, then left by a tiny lane past the Fox inn. Keep right when offered a choice of paths just ahead, cross a field and go through a belt of trees. Now at a large area of scrub, with the dark blur of trees on the far side of the valley ahead, keep left (leaving the main track) by a small footpath that runs down the field for some way before running ahead through another beechwood. Near the far side of the wood avoid a right fork and carry on to a stile at a field corner. The path runs on over a dip and by way of stiles over a large field to emerge at a lane by houses. Turn right downhill and in 100 yards take the field path on the left that runs half-right to reach the Shoulder of Mutton by **Wendover** station.

Getting there

Wendover: British Rail from Marylebone.

 Underground from Baker Street (change to B.R. at Amersham).

Butler's Cross: Bee Line bus 323 from Aylesbury via Great Kimble, to Princes Risborough and High Wycombe.

Car parking: car park off Wendover High Street.

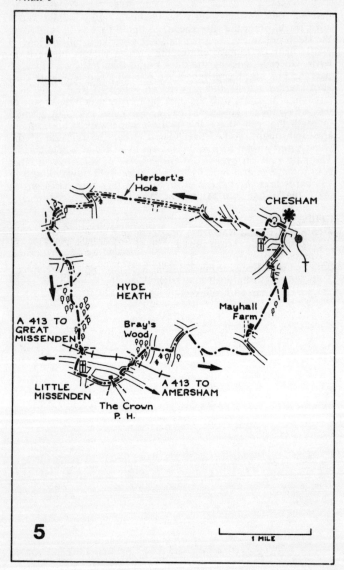

N

Herbert's Hole

CHESHAM

HYDE HEATH

Mayhall Farm

A 413 TO GREAT MISSENDEN

Bray's Wood

A 413 TO AMERSHAM

LITTLE MISSENDEN

The Crown P. H.

5

1 MILE

Walk 5. Chesham bottoms

Circular tour from Chesham through Hyde Heath to Little Missenden (9 miles).

This walk from Chesham, a town in the deeply-folded valley beside the river Chess, sets out to explore the series of long, dry valleys (dry because of the chalk below) that are typical of the Chiltern country around Chesham and Little Missenden. Again a church is the focal point of the tour — Little Missenden church has an especially important series of wall paintings discovered in the 1930s, which encouraged other church authorities to see what might lie beneath the limewash of the Victorian age.

The walk starts at Chesham, from the Star Yard car park by the Broadway, on the gyratory traffic system. Cross over the road to the recreation ground and walk towards the church.

However, before reaching the church turn right, following a drive that runs along the far side of the park, and keep uphill beside the hedge, when the drive turns away, with the open grass on your right. The grassy path finally dives through the trees, falling leftwards to cross two stiles and reach a field. Go half-left down the slope to a kissing-gate, cross the road and take the field path bearing half-right (signposted to 'Dry Dell') that leads to a wooden stile on the far side. Cross, and go slightly left now to a lane, then right for 200 yards to take the second track on the left, a long Chiltern 'bottom; known as **Herbert's Hole.** This track runs along the valley; after three-quarters of a mile when the made-up track turns left, keep forward by a field gate to follow the grassy valley path. After 200 yards go through a wooden swing-gate to pass to the right of a copse, then through an iron gate and so on to a road where you turn sharp left, uphill. Near the top of the rise take a concreted farm track on the right. Follow the path off right around paddocks and farmhouse, crossing the stile at the end of the paddocks to a wooden fence where turn right to a wooden gate at the start of a wood. Enter the wood and follow a faint path that runs not far from its right side. Buried deep in the trees are the once impressive ramparts of an old 'fosse'. Soon your path becomes a clear track that turns around the side of the wood. Ignore a path on the right by a white house and keep ahead to a shallow ditch-rampant to reach a hedged track which breaks out a wide gravelly drive near some bungalows.

The hedged footpath which leads on to **Hyde Heath** starts about 50 yards to the right along the lane just beyond the last bungalow (at present) called The Huddle. Turn left along this pretty path to a stile, keep beside the hedge to another gate-cum-stile attractively framed by the overhanging branches of a

33

wayside tree, and follow the wire fence (right) to go over another rustic barrier, where you bear slightly left, over grass, to the main road, opposite Hyde Lane.

About 50 yards to the left is the drive to The Hyde. Go past the white posts and along the approach. (Note the attractive lodge house in sham Tudor.) When the drive turns keep forward by a hedged path to a stile, and on to cross the girth of a long narrow field to a stile overlooking a large field with a depression running along its centre. Aiming to pass near the left edge of the line of wood opposite, strike downhill and upward, to the far corner at the end of the wood ahead — **Hedgemoor Wood.**

The path leads on, through a gap, just inside the left edge of the wood for 30 yards or so before breaking out into the field on the left. Keeping your direction, follow the hedge round — it soon runs leftwards — and when it bends right again cross the waist of the field to the wood on the far side. Now, as you turn downhill with the wood on your left, there are views across the Misbourne valley towards Holmer Green and Mop End. The path, becoming a clear track when the trees end, turns squarely left and runs across a little valley and up through a plantation. When a grassy track crosses your path turn right along it, passing through young mixed woodland. Ignore crossing tracks and follow your path downwards to a gate near a bridge and cross the railway. From the swing gate beyond go forward over a field to the main road and on along the hedge-side path opposite that crosses the bed of the Misbourne (it is often dry) to **Little Missenden** church.

LITTLE MISSENDEN. The church of St. John the Baptist dates back to Saxon times. The uncovering of the giant figure of St. Christopher (as well as other, smaller, wall paintings) aroused much interest just before the Second World War. Although now of lesser significance in the yearly calendar due to the recent papal ruling, St. Christopher was a popular saint because of his protection of wayfarers and it is interesting to note that this painting, in its earthy colours, is the only painting visible from outside the church, as it directly faces the door in invitation. The altar stone was buried at the time of the Reformation, and was only rediscovered by chance. The village has many interesting houses from the Georgian age. You will see these as you walk past the church and along the village street. Note especially the mill near the by-pass.

Keep ahead by the road passing Missenden House and the Crown to the by-pass again, cross to the slip road opposite and take the footpath starting a little to the right. This runs from a stile (farm left) up the side of a field to another stile and then by a small fenced path to the latticed railway footbridge, typical of the Metropolitan Railway's design.

On the far side to a stile at the edge of **Bray's Wood** and follow a clear track (at first to the right of a depression) through the beeches. This wood has been largely felled; the path turns right and then bears left, with an open area on the left for much of the time. Finally it winds right to a lane; cross to the gap opposite and follow a small hedge-side path that skirts an avenue of trees before turning to a stile, right. Cross the stile in the wire fence and keep ahead — still generally parallel with the hedgeline on the left — through scrub and on through a belt of trees to a road where you turn left for a quarter-mile to a signposted junction.

From the stile on the right continue between open fields and cross a stile into an area of small trees and growth that was until only a few years ago **Weedonhill Wood.** Keep on the track that runs uphill to pass below farm buildings, then on, along the top of the rise, all the way to a field. Keep on by the path across the field and so by a track to a road where you turn left for 500 yards to a track on the right, at cottages, leading to **Mayhall Farm.**

Just before the farm, turn right by a track that runs out to a crossing track near houses. Now go left, downhill, crossing a stile into a field on the left as the path turns after 300 yards or so. Strike very slightly right to a stile by a thicket and cross a field ahead slantwise to a corner gate and on, bearing slightly left to an estate road, when you turn left and round to a lane ahead leading down to Chesham High Street.

CHESHAM, with beech woods on all sides, has long been a centre of a thriving woodware industry. Although still expanding, the town has fine examples of seventeenth century buildings and the town hall, church and manor house form a pleasing group. The church of St. Mary was extensively restored in the late nineteenth century. There are several ancient inns to be seen near the High Street.

Getting there

Chesham: Underground from Baker Street or British Rail from Marylebone (change at Chalfont).

London Country buses from Berkhamsted (354); Watford (336); Gerrards Cross, Slough, Windsor (353); High Wycombe (362).

Little Missenden: London Country 359 to Amersham or Great Missenden.

Car parking: Chesham and en route.

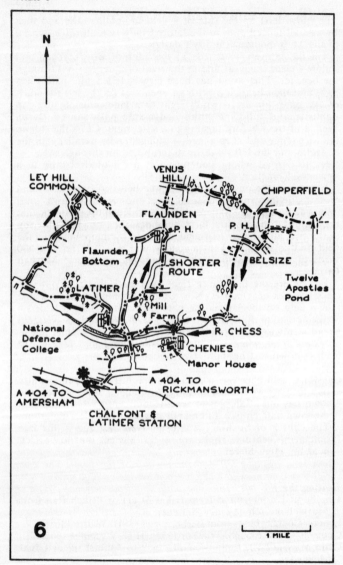

N

LEY HILL COMMON

VENUS HILL

CHIPPERFIELD

FLAUNDEN
P. H.

P. H.

Flaunden Bottom

SHORTER ROUTE

BELSIZE

LATIMER

Twelve Apostles Pond

Mill Farm

National Defence College

R. CHESS

CHENIES

Manor House

A 404 TO AMERSHAM

A 404 TO RICKMANSWORTH

CHALFONT & LATIMER STATION

6

1 MILE

Walk 6. Venus Hill and Twelve Apostles

Chalfont & Latimer station via Latimer, Ley Hill, Flaunden, Chipperfield, Belsize, Chenies and Latimer Bottom (12 or 9½ miles).

On the eastern side of the river Chess the meadowland keeps its freshness all the year. This walk traces out some of the waterside paths after climbing the high ground to Flaunden and Venus Hill. A number of different routes can be taken to fit in with the distance you wish to walk — directly to Flaunden or by detour to Chenies — but try to reach the tranquil beauty of the Twelve Apostles pond, set deep in the woods of Chipperfield Common. A link with Chalfont & Latimer station is included for walkers arriving by train; see the end of the walk for car parking suggestions.

From **Chalfont & Latimer** station's main entrance, walk uphill and take the second turning on the left, Chessfield Park, serving new houses. Keep forward as it turns at the end and along the right of a playing field to a stile where you turn right along a cross track that keeps to the high ground. At a lane, go downhill and cross the lower road to reach a little bridge spanning the Chess. Carry on to the triangular green at **Latimer,** a short distance ahead, where you can, if you wish, shorten the distance to Flaunden.

LATIMER village, drowsing in the valley of the Chess, is a place of quiet cottages enclosing a tiny green on which there is a canopied pump (a reminder of the days before piped water when much of the village gossip would be retailed as the villagers gathered to fill their buckets), a small memorial to the village war dead and a cairn marking the burial place of a horse! It was the resting place of the favourite hunter of the Boer General Viljoen and seems strangely out of place here.

(For the short alternative walk to Flaunden, carry on by the road past a farm to a track, starting from a wooden field gate on the right, that climbs up the hill, bearing left and then turning right (you avoid a left path at the top of the field). The clear bridleway continues to reach a broad avenue on high ground, with a wood on the left. Take the path that leads left here, running round the wood with a plantation on your right, which later runs as a farm track towards Martin's Top Farm ahead. Do not go right to the farm, but take the signposted path on the left. Go leftwards by the path, along the side of the field to an observatory. Here the path turns left for a few yards before resuming its direction and, as a surfaced lane, running on to emerge at Flaunden church. Keep forward to the

gate ahead and follow the directions from page 39.)

To continue the main walk, turn left at the green and go forward, as the road bends away, up the grassy footpath starting from a step between two cottages. By way of swing gates you come to a road on higher ground. Now turn right until the road bears right near a post-box. Leave the road and keep ahead, between two blocks, to a stile, then follow the left side of a large field (with a wood on the left) to the far side. A footpath starting from the corner runs under trees, with wire fencing right, to emerge quickly to give one of the very finest views of the river Chess. The grassy way now drops to end at a small swing-gate at a field; keep the hedge on the left through three fields to reach barns at a lane.

The pretty lane, enclosed by high hedges, climbs steeply to the right; leave it at a sharp right turn to cross a stile directly ahead. You are now in a field on high ground; keep the same direction over the grass (or follow the left hedgeline if in crop) over the rising ground aiming generally for the tops of trees on the far side. In 300 yards cross a stile in the hedge, and another a few feet away, and go forward over a second field to reach a lane by a wooden gate just right of the white house ahead. Keep forward still, pass the house and follow this pleasant rural way (you will be unlucky indeed to meet a car) to its junction with the Ley Hill road, which leads leftwards past a few cottages to another road junction in a hollow. Take the right fork (marked Bovingdon) which soon climbs up to the open grassland on the side of **Ley Hill Common.**

LEY HILL COMMON is a stretch of hill-top almost 500 feet high. On the far side of the golf course (left) are a few scattered houses and an inn. The Hertfordshire boundary is only half a mile away, on the far side of the ridge.

On meeting another road near the golf club car park, turn right and, after 200 yards as you reach a bend, leftwards through a wide gap into a field. A broad track follows the side of the field for 100 yards or so, then swings right, following the high Chiltern spur. After three-quarters of a mile the way falls, with the path now following a left-hand hedge through which come glimpses of a chalk-pit. Finally you turn left to a road bend at **Flaunden Bottom,** the Hertfordshire boundary. After climbing the hill you reach **Flaunden.** (The church, right, is an early work of Sir Gilbert Scott, built in 1838 to replace Flaunden Old

Church which you will pass later.) *Here short-distance walkers rejoin the walk.* As the road turns right at the top of the hill, go leftwards over a gate and along the right side of fields and between gardens to the Boxmoor road. A tiny path from a stile 100 yards to the left and on the far side of the road (opposite a bungalow called Roydon) leads on to Venus Hill; it is an unkempt path at first that passes a caravan site.

On reaching the tiny by-lane (**Venus Hill**), go right to the main road again. On the way you pass Austin's Hall Farm, a very handsome timber-framed farmhouse and, a little further on, Venus Hill Farm — an L-shaped building that has mellowed well.

From the gate (marked with a sign) almost opposite the T-junction ahead, go uphill over a field that broadens near the top. The path near the left side of the field runs under the overhanging branches of beech trees and on through another field to reach another tiny lane, where you turn right. The lanes around Flaunden have long been well-known for hedges of holly and soon this quiet backwater is shielded by tall green banks giving it a Christmas-card appearance. Leave the lane as it makes a sharp right turn and cross over a stile which is beside a wire gate on the left. Ignoring a left-hand track at once, keep straight on through the groves of a plantation by the clear forward path. After dropping to pass a barrier in a small vale, bear very *slightly* right to use the footpath (not the horse track) that skirts the edge of the mature trees (a waymark sign gives the direction). After crossing the horse track, the footpath climbs up by a plantation to run out later at a stile by a farm track. Cross and follow the left side of a field to a road at **Chipperfield,** where you go left, uphill and then first right at a road at the edge of the common's trees.

Now take the signposted bridle-track on the right, only a few yards from the junction, that traces the right side of the common, emerging soon near houses (right) and running on under the trees to another wide area, with houses nearby. The track keeps ahead, soon returning to the shade of the trees. In 150 yards or so you will note an iron gate and bar stile on your right — the walk returns to this point. In another quarter-mile the trees on your left part to disclose the **Pond of the Twelve Apostles,** a well-loved pool in the woods. The 'apostles' are the twelve beeches that encompass the water; eleven are ancient, the other is a replacement, very much younger.

Retrace your steps along the border track to the iron gate and stile, and cross to a good hedged track that leads to a lane at a bend. The path on the right — a gravel track marked 'Footpath' — leads on for 600 yards to a road junction, with the Plough Inn at **Belsize** away on the right.

The walk continues across the road to Poles Hill, half-left, which runs uphill to reach a small lane meeting it on the right. Turn along this ridge-top lane — there are wide views to the right towards Bovingdon — until you reach a footpath sign-posted 'Chenies' on the left at the start of a small wood. You follow the side of a large field, divided with wire, over stiles to reach a farm drive, with the farmhouse on the right. Cross the drive and skirt around the corrugated-iron barn ahead and follow the footpath signs to pick up a well-used field track that hugs a hedge at first, then strikes forward across the field to the hedge on the far side. Here the path runs on to become a pretty woodland track that runs downward, soon turning into a sunken way that suggests great age. Continue on near the depression all the way down until the wood ends. Now the path breaks out into the open to show you, again, the Chess valley. When the path expires at a farm go downhill to the water and a footbridge.

The return path to Latimer now keeps closely beside the untidy banks of the river; cross the bar stile, *before* the footbridge, into a field on the right. Here a path runs over grass, with the water on the left, to a stile, across another field to a hedge where turn right alongside and into a small wood to a stile. With the white farmhouse in the distance as your next objective, go on across the grass to a stile at a lane, then left to pass the building, Mill Farm.

At this point a detour can be made to the village of **Chenies**, the sister village of Latimer, perched on the hill just inside Buckinghamshire and beyond the stream. The village is reached by a footpath that starts opposite the road junction beyond the farm. The path (take the left-hand one at the road) runs up near the side of the wood, bearing leftward to clear the trees at the top and running on to Chenies Manor House.

CHENIES. The great House of Chenies, with its red-brick collection of twisted chimneys and gables, was the home of the
Russell family, Dukes of Bedford. The Bedford chapel in
Chenies church is a vast treasure-house of funeral
monuments; among those buried here was Lord John Russell,
the Victorian statesman. The mansion is typically Tudor and
date from 1532. In the words of Froude, in his *Cheneys and
House of Russell* 'Cheneys, its red gable-ends and its venera-
ble trees ... is pervaded by an aspect of serene good manners
as if it were always Sunday.'

The main walk continues from Mill Farm by the path which runs straight through the farmyard, turns left for a yard or so nearer the stream, then runs parallel to the river, shortly passing between hedges and on to a gate. Here, at a field, the grassy path continues ahead to pass the lonely tomb of Alice and William Liberty, a freethinker (as he was described) who asked to be buried here, away from the church that once stood just away to your left, in 1777. This was **Flaunden Old Church**, thankfully abandoned when the new church was built on higher ground almost a mile away. The path goes forward along the centre of a grassy field. Continue to the road where turn left and retrace your steps to **Chalfont & Latimer** station.

Getting there
Chalfont & Latimer: British Rail from Marylebone, Underground from Baker Street.
Chenies: London Country bus 336 from Watford and Rickmansworth to Amersham and Chesham.
Ley Hill: London Country bus 336 from Chesham.
Car parking: Chipperfield Common, Ley Hill or Latimer.

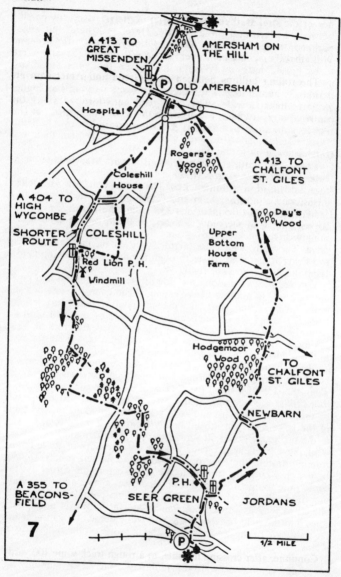

Walk 7. The Amersham scene

Circular tour from Seer Green (or Amersham) via Newbarn, Amersham, Coleshill and Poland Green (10¼ miles).

The rolling hilltops between Seer Green and Amersham give splendid vantage points to survey the finest parts of the Chiltern country near London. This walk is planned from Seer Green station, but instructions are given so that it can be carried out from Amersham, easily reached by Underground or British Rail train from London. Short-distance walkers can easily plan their walk from one station to the other.

From **Seer Green** station follow the path leftwards from the opposite side of the car park, soon bearing right, downhill, across a road, and on up over another road to the school. Now keep ahead in the road almost to the church, Holy Trinity, which was built in 1846. The stony track that starts on the right just *before* the tiny Baptist chapel at the road fork here is the first path to take. The shingly drive quickly splits — take the path to the left of the farm drive. The path, with close-boarded fencing on the right, leads to two fields at first, and passes through the hedge at a playing field to bring the bushes to your right.

You keep forward along the side of the sports ground and on by the right side of another field, keeping ahead over the grass to a stile in the far hedgeline. Here, at a meeting point of paths, turn left and keep the hedge on your left around the side of the field until the path becomes a track leading to a stile at a road. Chalfont St. Giles lies away to the right, but the walk turns leftwards along the road to the road junction ahead at **Newbarn.**

Leave the road immediately beyond the weatherboarded barns of Newbarn Farm, on the corner, and turn right, between white posts, along the side of a small paddock with stout fencing on your right, to a stile at the side of a field. Carry on beside the hedge to a stile on the left. Go over this and keep your direction along the right side of the large field you are in, finally bearing off leftwards to a gap in the far hedge about 50 yards from the right corner.

In the next field the path follows the contours of its left side, running around the edge of a wood to the far left corner. Do not be tempted by paths turning to the wood before the corner. At the corner, the footpath enters the wood, crosses a stile, and runs inside the right edge of Hodgemoor Wood. This path leads generally ahead; as long as you do not wander too far leftwards, and ignore stiles into the field on your right, you will emerge at a gap near the far right side of the wood, with a stile opposite on the other side of a lane.

Continue, after crossing the stile, to a rough track some 100 yards ahead and continue forward downhill past some untidy buildings on your right. Avoid a right fork and your track will lead to **Upper Bottom Farm** — in a valley but, as its name implies, on higher ground than its neighbour, Lower Bottom Farm, away on the Amersham road to the right. (You may have to climb a rough gate before reaching the farm.) Cross directly over the lane through a farmyard and up out of the valley.

Soon, high up on the grassy downland, you have views far over the Misbourne valley. Near the top of the hill, the fieldside path meets a gate; cross into the field on the left and continue over the rising ground along the left side of the field, near clumps of hawthorn, to a stile set in the hedge some 30 yards from the far corner. Beyond the stile you are in a field over 400 feet high. Go half right to a stile in the far corner beyond the brow of the hill, leaving Day's Wood on your right. Here the views open towards Amersham, with Amersham-on-the-Hill and the railway station on the far rise.

For 80 yards or so the line of the hedge guides you forward; when it turns towards the farm, continue across the field to a corner stile. Still continue forward to a stile at **Roger's Wood**, set about 100 yards from the far corner of the field.

Pass through the wood to reach a sloping field, and continue half leftwards to a stile in the far left hedge some way from the corner. The path now runs clearly downhill, by way of another stile, to reach a track which passes under the bypass and reaches the main road at **Bury Farm**. (For walkers who seek the quickest way to **Amersham** station, turn right to the roundabout and up the hill.)

To join the walk from Amersham station you must reach the Old Town, in the valley. From the main station entrance, turn left under the railway bridge, then along the path on the right. Take the clear track on the left, just before reaching a road, through Parsonage Wood and down over a field, bearing left at a wall, then right to the churchyard, to Amersham main street.

OLD AMERSHAM'S main street has retained its character in spite of increased traffic. The Town Hall, built by Sir William Drake in the seventeenth century, remains stubbornly in the centre of the street on its rounded arches. The Drake family owned Shardeloes House, the large mansion just beyond Amersham which can be glimpsed from Walk 5 in this book. Amersham was important in the days of the stage-coach and several fine coaching inns on both sides of the Town Hall mark their presence with large gaily-painted signs.

Take the Beachfield road (left at the Gore Hall roundabout) and before the next roundabout cross the road to the footbridge ahead, walk across and turn right. Follow the signposted footpath up the slope keeping to the bank and bearing slightly right. Once over the hill, follow the path to a lodge (ignore the path to the water tower), turn right then left, beside a line of six oaks and ashes, and ascend the hill to the pylon, where take the left gate to a field. The path runs past farm buildings to a road at a bend. Here you may save time by continuing ahead through Coleshill, resuming the instructions at the village notes below.

The route of the walk bears leftwards, past the beautiful front of Coleshill House, to the sharp road bend. Here turn right through a gate and follow the path alongside the hedge for three fields and continue until you cross a field path waymarked white on a stile in the left-hand fence. Here turn right across the field towards a small wood in the distance, reaching another field through two wooden posts. The path bears right for a few yards around the trees before reaching a shady track at a stile. Carry on to reach **Coleshill** village at the Red Lion.

COLESHILL village formed a detached part of Hertfordshire (surrounded by Buckinghamshire) until 1831. As early as the days of Edward I, in the thirteenth century, it was in Hertfordshire, being transferred by an Act of William IV. The historian Chauncy, writing in 1700, explained that it was the custom for a sheriff to ask the monarch to append land owned by the administrator in another county to his larger area; if so, such a practice has led to constant boundary alterations over the centuries and is marked, in the case of Coleshill, by at least one local mansion bearing the old county name. The village was called Old Stoke in the days of the poet Edmund Waller. He was born here.

As you walk past the pond and through the village to the edge of the ridge on which Coleshill stands, note the old tower windmill, on the left. It is a brick structure which still possesses its wooden cap, although the main sails have gone. The windmill dates from 1856.

The road falls beyond Glebe House to a junction, where a footpath immediately ahead leads through a small copse to a farm drive. Turn right and after fifty yards cross over a stile on the left near a pylon line and follow the general line of the wires to a stile that brings you into a field with trees and farm on your right. Leave the field through the iron swing-gate in the far corner, bear left for a few yards to a wood, then bear along the side of the field, keeping the trees on your left, and through steel posts when the wood ends. The path now turns into another wood and cuts a corner of the wood to a cross track in the valley below. (The path can be elusive but helpful white paint marks on strategically placed trees may guide your steps.)

The broad bridle track now leads the way leftwards; after 200 yards leave it at signposted cross tracks to cross a stile on the right and follow a hedge-side path to another track at an area of higher ground known as **Poland Green**. Keep left, and after crossing the main road, continue by a hedged track directly opposite for 200 yards until it runs down to a valley where a footpath starts on the right at a gate. Go through the gate into a dense plantation of young fir, relieved by the feathery delicate fronds of an occasional larch. At another gate go left for a few yards to a sloping field, but follow the right (lower) side, soon entering another plantation until you reach a wide avenue between older trees at the end of the left-hand field. Go left now, over the stile up the side of the field and half-right by the clear path in a higher field to reach houses at a lane on the far side. After turning left, go first right (Orchard Road), which runs shortly to **Seer Green,** with the church ahead. Pass the church on the left and turn right to pass the Baptist Chapel a few yards away. The road leads to Seer Green station, as on the outward journey; if you joined the walk at Amersham or points on the way, turn along the gravel track on the left, just beyond the chapel and follow the instructions at the start of the walk.

Getting there

Seer Green: British Rail from Marylebone.

London Country bus 305, from Uxbridge and Gerrards Cross to Beaconsfield and High Wycombe.

Coleshill: London Country bus 398 from Amersham and High Wycombe.

Amersham: British Rail from Marylebone. Underground from Baker Street.

London Country buses from Berkhamstead (354); Watford (336); Windsor and Slough (353); High Wycombe (362).

Walk 8. Ashridge and Aldbury

Circular tour from Berkhamsted by way of Nettleden, Little Gaddesden, Aldbury and Northchurch (11½ miles).

The Bridgewater Monument, a 100-foot Doric column to the memory of the pioneer canal builder, is in more than one sense the high point of this varied walk. But the Duke of Bridgewater, pioneer of the canal age of the late eighteenth century that paved the way for the Industrial Revolution, has a social monument of lasting value in the Grand Union Canal itself. Little Gaddesden church, rich in memorials to the Bridgewater family, should be visited, but leave yourself time to see the other churches, all with interesting monuments, which lie along the route. An all season walk just inside Hertfordshire, like all Chiltern walks, best undertaken under the golden tints of autumn.

BERKHAMSTED is a prosperous country town in the Bulbourne valley. The Norman castle was built by Earl Mortain, brother of William the Conqueror, and was a royal residence (favoured by the Black Prince) for about 400 years; its banks, grounds and ruined walls are now in the care of the Department of the Environment. The thirteenth century St. Peter's church, one of the largest in the county, contains many brasses and monuments dating from the fourteenth century. Berkhamsted's grammar school was founded by John Incent, Dean of St. Pauls, in 1544. The Foundling Hospital, founded in 1739 by Thomas Coram of Bloomsbury, now occupies a modern building in the grounds of Ashlyn Hall. In the High Street, amid some very odd relics of the Victorian age, are some pretty half-timbered cottages and almshouses dating from the seventeenth century.

The walk starts from **St. Peter's church** in the High Street. (Walkers arriving by railway walk forward to New Road.) Walk down Castle Street and turn right at the bottom to pass under the railway arch and take New Road, which skirts the right edge of the castle grounds. After about 200 yards, at the end of a large field on the right, and roughly level with the end of the castle's ruined walls, a footpath sign at a stile directs up the hill to the right. Climb up over grass (fencing right) to another stile and on to the top of the rise. As you turn left along the top of the field you will see most of Berkhamsted nestling in the valley floor of the Bulbourne. The path crosses stiles, skirts the Wellcombe Foundation, to a stile ahead, beside a stone-and-brick wall bowing with age. Beyond the stile, the path winds quickly round to a gravel track that leads, with a golf clubhouse on the right, to a road.

47

Turn left for 50 yards or so to the war memorial obelisk opposite a road junction on the right. A clear bridleway, starting from the memorial, leads across the golf course. After crossing the first fairway the path splits at a signpost. Turn off by the left-hand path (signposted 'Footpath only') and follow it ahead across the rest of the course and on by an enclosed path between houses lining the edge of the common. The path crosses a by-road and continues, enclosed by the fencing of a couple of houses, until it widens and leads very clearly through rough woodland. Later the track falls to a lane opposite some pretty cottages; here you turn right to **Frithsden**, a tiny huddle of interesting old houses and farms grouped around the Alford Arms. Take a road on the left at the inn, marked 'Unsuitable for motor vehicles'. This sunken track, known as the Old Roman Road, takes you over a steep hill to **Nettleden.**

NETTLEDEN is a charming tiny village with some Tudor houses in the fold of the hills. The church, St. Lawrence, was rebuilt in brick during Georgian times, but the tower is fifteenth century flint. A fine avenue of clipped yews leads to the porch. There is a splendid brass to John Cotton, dated from 1545, and a seventeenth century monument to Edmund Bressy.

Take the small path that starts about 20 yards to the left of your arrival track, immediately left of the building opposite. It climbs out of the valley with wire fencing and a field to your left, passes to the right of the Amaraviti Buddhist Centre at the top of the hill, then beside a right-hand hedge, forward to a tiny ridge-top lane. (For faint hearts who prefer a hard surface the lane opposite Nettleden church leads also to the hill-top lane.) Turn left on the lane, which loses its surface to become a rough track.

After passing some pretty backwater cottages, the track runs half a mile to **Hudnall Common** National Trust land, where there is a good view towards the wooded hills beyond the valley of the Gade.

After passing Hudnall Farm (left) you arrive at crossroads. Go straight ahead on a road which, 200 yards on, bears left then right. Where it bears right, keep forward to an enclosed path on the left (beside an ornamental lamp) leading to a wicket gate opening on to a field. Now follow the hedge-side path, cross a stile and go forward through a large field to a fence. The high ridge to your right is part of Dunstable Downs; Whipsnade Park Zoo is laid out on the slopes.

Now cross into the next field and strike half-left to **Little Gaddesden church.**

LITTLE GADDESDEN CHURCH is fifteenth century and dedicated to

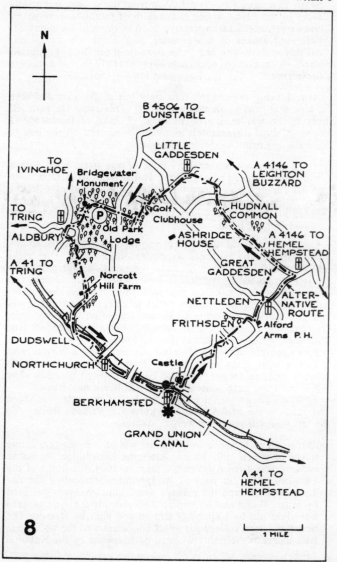

N

B 4506 TO DUNSTABLE

LITTLE GADDESDEN

A 4146 TO LEIGHTON BUZZARD

TO IVINGHOE

Bridgewater Monument

TO TRING

ALDBURY

P

Golf Clubhouse

HUDNALL COMMON

Old Park Lodge

ASHRIDGE HOUSE

A 4146 TO HEMEL HEMPSTEAD

A 41 TO TRING

Norcott Hill Farm

GREAT GADDESDEN

NETTLEDEN

ALTER-NATIVE ROUTE

FRITHSDEN

Alford Arms P. H.

DUDSWELL

NORTHCHURCH

Castle

BERKHAMSTED

GRAND UNION CANAL

A 41 TO HEMEL HEMPSTEAD

8

1 MILE

Saints Peter and Paul, is detached from the village, and stands alone in the fields. Inside is a wealth of monuments of many types (repainted quite recently), most of them to the Egertons, Earls and Dukes of Bridgewater, and former owners of the Ashridge estate. The 3rd Duke (who built the canals) is buried here. A masterpiece in white marble by Westacott commemorates the 7th Earl, who rebuilt Ashridge.

After leaving the church turn right out of the gate and take the lane that runs to the main road 700 yards away. On your left there is the war memorial in front of John of Gaddesden's House. A short distance left along the road, and off the line of the walk, is Little Gaddesden village.

LITTLE GADDESDEN is a pretty village of one street lined with a wide grass verge. The old Manor House dates from 1576. John of Gaddesden was a court physician and friend of Chaucer and is mentioned in *Canterbury Tales*. The present half-timbered fifteenth century building replaced the one in which he is said to have lived.

Cross the road at the war memorial and pass through the white gates at the entrance to the Ashridge estate. Turn right into Ringshall Drive after 70 yards. 150 yards on, take a drive on the left signposted to Witches Hollow. Where it divides into two private driveways, take an enclosed path between them. This path climbs out of the shallow valley to emerge at a golf fairway and continues as a bridleway between trees on the other side. On reaching a metalled road, turn left then right, then left past 'Pitstone Copse' on a road to the clubhouse.

Pass the right of the clubhouse buildings, cross a fairway, and follow a wide grass track to **Old Park Lodge,** a seventeenth century hunting lodge. Note the curious twisted chimney. The 7th Duke lived here while Ashridge was being modernised.

Follow a rough gravel path to the left of the lodge for about 150 yards to the broad grass ride known as Prince's Riding. To the left you will see the towers of **Ashridge.**

ASHRIDGE. The house is built on the site of a monastery, some traces of which still remain. After the Dissolution the house became first a royal residence then, in 1604, the home of the Egertons. The 7th Earl of Bridgewater demolished the old house and ordered the present neo-Gothic mansion designed by James Wyatt and his son Sir Jeffry Wyattville. The gardens were laid out by Capability Brown and later by Repton. The house is now a college for adult education and the public has free access to the richly wooded park, owned by the National Trust.

To your right, nearly a mile away, your next objective is clearly visible. Turn right and walk to it.

THE BRIDGEWATER MONUMENT. Built in memory of the canal-building Duke of Bridgewater. In summer, it is well worth the climb of 170 steps inside, on a payment at the tea cottage, for a wonderful view over the edge of the chalk scarp. The tea cottage, by the way, is closed on Fridays and during the winter.

Turn left at the monument and follow the rough gravel path in front of the tea cottage. This path plunges down through magnificent beech trees. Ignore a left fork on the way and you will emerge at **Aldbury.**

ALDBURY. Half-timbered cottages, some thatched, face the charming pond and village green, where stocks and a whipping post still stand. In the parish church is the marble tomb of Sir Ralph Verney, ancestor of Charles I's standard-bearer at Edgehill. There are some splendid monuments in the Pendley chapel.

Turn left at the pond and left again at the Valiant Trooper. Turn left up Malting Lane where the main road bends right. Beyond the houses, this lane turns left, and on the right is a narrow chalky path leading up through the woods. This path brings you to a road. Turn right, and carry on by a lane where the main road turns left. Watch for a path on the left on a bend after about 100 yards. Follow this path through the fern for 150 yards or so, avoiding all tempting paths leading leftwards into the common, to a gateside stile. Cross the stile and follow a hedge-side path forward to the far corner of the field. Here you will find a stile, a kissing gate and another stile on the right. Negotiate all three, and continue in the same direction with first a wire fence and then a hedge on your left. At last cross a stile by a metal field-gate and follow a drive past the handsome neo-Queen Anne **Norcott Hill Farm.** Follow the road from here down the scarp to the Grand Union Canal at **Dudswell,** ignoring a right fork on the way. Turn left along the canal towpath for the final easy stroll back towards Northchurch and Berkhamsted.

If you prefer to return to **Northchurch,** leave the towpath at the next road bridge and turn right for Green Line coaches or buses.

NORTHCHURCH. The church of St. Mary is flint, with a Totternhoe stone crossing tower. Parts of the wall are Saxon.

There is a brass tablet to Peter the Wild Boy, who was found in the woods near Hanover and brought to England by Queen Caroline in 1725. He died nearby when about 72, having defied all attempts to educate him.

Getting there

Berkhamsted: British Rail from Euston.

Green Line coach 708 from London (Victoria) via Watford and Hemel Hempstead to Aylesbury.

London Country buses from Watford and Hemel Hempstead (301, 302); Windsor, Slough, Gerrards Cross, Amersham, Chesham (354); Tring, Aylesbury (301).

Northchurch: Green Line coach 708, London to Aylesbury.

London Country buses 301, 302 from Watford and Hemel Hempstead; 301 from Aylesbury.

Aldbury: London Country bus 387 from Tring.

Car parking: Ashridge, Aldbury and en route.

Walk 9. Georgian frolics

Circular walk from Marlow by way of Forty Green, Davenport Wood, Medmenham Camp, Medmenham, Harleyford Manor and the riverside (8 or 6 miles).

This walk covers the beautiful reaches of the Thames beyond Marlow, journeying over the wooded slopes above the river to visit Medmenham, a small village near the water that acquired a slightly sinister reputation during the eighteenth century as the scene of nefarious revelries by a group of fashionable men. The return is easy, over paths that keep to the level ground near the river.

A suggestion for reducing the walk to one that can be carried out in an afternoon is made in the description. It is a pleasant walk that belongs to all seasons.

MARLOW. A small pleasant town beside the Thames, well remembered by motorists for its narrow suspension bridge over the river, erected in 1832 to the designs of Clark, the architect of a suspension bridge at Hammersmith. The church is of no architectural merit, but contains some interesting monuments, notably one to Sir Miles Hobart who was killed in a coach accident in 1632. Shelley lived in Marlow and composed *Revolt of Islam* whilst he lay in his bobbing boat moored nearby.

From **Marlow** station walk up to the High Street, and take the lane directly opposite. (If you come by car or bus, this is the lane on the right at the river end of the High Street, not far from the church.) It passes public toilets and a large car park on the left — a convenient place for 'motorist' walkers to leave their vehicle. A footpath starts from iron bars on the right, opposite the car park; follow this to the main road, and continue along another road just a few yards to the right and on the far side (Oxford Road). After 200 yards or so from the junction and after passing the Crown and Anchor, turn left along a little tarmac path that winds upwards around some playing fields to cross a new residential road. Steps opposite will allow you to continue uphill by the path, crossing two more side-roads. Continue up Terrington Hill opposite, follow it as it bears left and take the footpath on the right just before Conniston Close, with Spinfield School to your right and follow it around gardens to yet another residential road where you turn left to reach the Bovingdon Green road.

Still rising, this road takes you, to the right, to a footpath starting beside trees on the left side as the road turns slightly

53

(the path should be signposted and is almost opposite Boving-don Heights). Almost at once the footpath splits; bear to the right to reach a field and follow it over a field to a stile at the end of a hedge. Cross the stile and keep near the hedge on the right down a wonderful grassy valley which allows views, left, towards the river. Perhaps with justification the locals know this spot as the 'Happy Valley', Continue over a stile at the field corner in the floor of the valley; the clear path now continues beside a left-hand hedge to a sturdy stile at **Davenport Wood.** The pretty woodland path, which runs forward very clearly along the low ground, has a fork after 250 yards. Keep to the more clearly marked path, the left-hand one, and trace it out as it gently climbs through the trees bearing gradually leftwards to a wide track that takes you on not far from the left edge of the wood. There are occasional waymarks on trees and you should keep just inside the wood for another 250 yards to a road, near a junction on the left.

Go a few yards to the left to the signpost, and then along the crossing road for about the same distance to the right. Here, at the start of a wood on the left, is a footpath sign with two plates. The track used by the walk is marked '5' on the post; it starts about 15 yards beyond the post. This track, which runs quickly into the heart of the wood, is bold and straight at first. After 250 yards comes a clear fork — take the right-hand one (waymarked with white arrows). Now trace out the path, with the help of the arrows, as it runs for a short distance half-right, then swings back through a young plantation. The track does go obviously on to reach a crossing path after running near a strong stand of tall dark pine trees (on the right) **(1).**

The main walk turns right at the crossing to keep the tall pines on your right. Beyond these trees the path bears leftwards on a gravelled drive that runs out of the wood beside a house. Bear right, following the path along the boundary at the edge of the trees and so out to the start of a track near houses. The track runs downhill, later bearing right to strike the main Medmenham road beside an overbridge. It is worth noting that even if you do go wrong and finish up with the housing estate (the RAF married quarters) on your right — as you will if you are following the short walk — the main route can be picked up again easily by following the main road to the right until the overbridge is reached.

Now, go down the main road, turning sharply right after 200 yards along the private track to King's Barn Farm. At a group of three gates climb up to pass Pheasantry Cottage to a wooden field-gate where a track runs around a house or two to a good firm drive on higher ground which you follow to the right.

As you pass another group of houses on the right, which includes a former school, look for a path on the left that starts

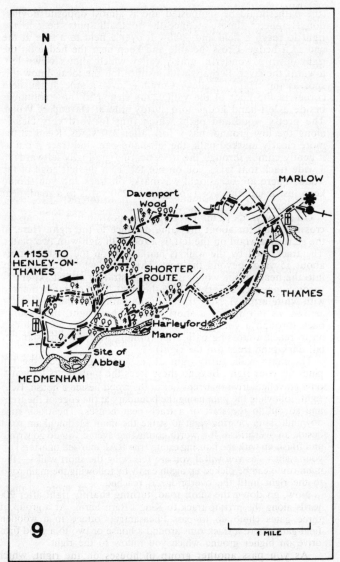

N

MARLOW

Davenport
Wood

A 4155 TO
HENLEY-ON-
THAMES

P.H.

SHORTER
ROUTE

R. THAMES

Harleyford
Manor

Site of
Abbey

MEDMENHAM

9   1 MILE

opposite the front door of the last house. Go over a wide drive and forward towards a meadow, but turn right, before reaching it, through an iron gate. This little woodland path leads around to the remains of an ancient Iron Age hill-fort. Trees grow over the whole area, but allow yourself to walk over the site until you are following a broad track that runs along the ramparts on the right side, with the land falling steeply away. Look for a smaller path as the track swings leftwards, and go down the plunging path until it runs out to a road far below, almost opposite **Medmenham** church and the main road. (There are buses from here back to Marlow.) Cross to the 'no through road' opposite.

MEDMENHAM. As you walk through the village, it will be clear that these lovely, abundantly restored cottages form the older part. The church, standing a half-mile from the river, is of little interest, although there is some Norman work around the south porch. Medmenham's claim to interest arises from Medmenham Abbey, near the river, which was founded by Isabel de Bolebec in 1204 and has totally disappeared. Its ruins attracted the interest of the Georgian high-society rakes who met there, mimicking the old religious rites. This group, which called itself the 'Monks of Medmenham Abbey', included Wilkes, the wit Charles Churchill, Sir Francis Dashwood of West Wycombe, and the dramatist Whitehead. Wilkes, at one meeting, released into the meeting a baboon, 'made up' as Satan.

Keep on past the post office until you cross a tiny brook as the lane turns slightly. On the far side of the bridge turn left at once along a private drive at Monks Cottage and continue along the footpath by the brook, over a footbridge (some care here) and then over a stile to a broad low-lying water meadow. Strike half-left, aiming just left of the centre group of trees, and on the far side cross a stile and bear left over a small stucco bridge to the main road again.

No more than 10 yards to the right is a drive which soon hurries away from the road. After passing a fine lodge house, the drive runs beneath the shelter of tall chalk cliffs which have been tunnelled by generations of animals. Next comes the broad sweep of the Thames — the path, lined with ancient iron pales, takes you past a Georgian riverside villa. Yet more strange things lie ahead: first the roar of a weir (which seems to remain always just out of sight); then, as the path turns away from the Thames, it passes through a long tunnel lit only fitfully by two glazing strips. Beyond, the path reaches a crossing track; here turn right.

(2) Continue beside the iron railings by the path which runs

downhill, then up to a wide meadow. Bear right, around the field, taking the broad field-edge path to pass a house then, as the track becomes a stone-clad drive, trace it around to pass the barns of Harleyford Manor farm.

HARLEYFORD MANOR, lying away to the right, and its estate are built in pleasing red brick. The house was erected in 1755 from designs by Sir Robert Taylor.

Now, as the drive turns sharply left, keep forward by a small path which drops to reach an approach drive below. Avoiding any paths leading uphill on the grass opposite, keep directly forward after crossing the drive — the footpath leads out to a field which is now a major holiday caravan site. For almost a half-mile the way lies ahead over the grass — just keep the trees of Home Copse on your left. On reaching a lodge (note the complexity of devices on the stucco), swing right along a rough farm track, soon passing the farm at Low Grounds. Just beyond the farm buildings comes a choice of paths back to Marlow. If you prefer the pleasant stroll back beside the river just follow the track round to cross the gate ahead, and keep forward to the towing path. It leads, to the left, all the way to Marlow, passing Bisham Abbey on the opposite bank.

For a slightly shorter route back, turn sharp left after the farm buildings along a field track marked by posts. The way leads quite straight for a mile, crossing only one stile, until it runs, as a bumpy stone track, into the lane that finally passes the car park near Marlow Bridge.

The short route

Follow the main walk to the end of the paragraph marked (1). At the crossing path by the pine trees, turn left (following arrows), and then quickly right until you run close to the housing estate on the right, going left of the buildings, the RAF married quarters, and finally bearing right to reach the main road by way of the service road to the houses. Cross directly over the main road to a signposted path on the far side. Now simply follow the path over the meadow ahead, aiming to the right of a clump of trees. The path crosses a drive, then runs on for some 30 yards until a junction of paths is reached. Now turn left, and rejoin the instructions for the main walk at the paragraph marked (2).

Getting there

Marlow: British Rail from Paddington, changing at Maidenhead. No service on Sundays.

Bee Line buses 328, 329 from High Wycombe, Henley and

Reading. Alder Valley bus 18 from Maidenhead.
Medmenham: Bee Line buses 328, 329, High Wycombe-Marlow-Henly-Reading.
Wycombe-Marlow-Henley-Reading.
Car parking: Marlow.

Walk 10. Remote Chiltern villages

Circular walk from Ibstone Common by way of Turville (and Fingest), and Ibstone (7 miles), with linked circuit from Stokenchurch to Ibstone Common and return (10 miles).

This walk explores the deep folds of the Buckinghamshire Chilterns that run, in tumbles, westwards from Wycombe. It is beautiful in all seasons, but at no time is it more attractive than in autumn, when the beech 'carpet' turns from deep gold and red to become brown. In this russet-tinted wonderland a little distance, so to speak, goes a long way, and you may care to use Ibstone Common for a starting point, although the walk, as can be seen from the map, can be done as a 'figure-of-eight' from Stokenchurch. Follow the walk from the paragraph marked (1) if you are trying the short tour.

STOKENCHURCH has now had its traffic problems solved at the expense of having a motorway just beyond its main street. It is a large village on one of the highest points of the Chilterns and has for many years been associated with chair-making. The church contains two interesting late brasses; they depict members of the Tipping family and date from 1632. The Morle brasses (c. 1400) have inscriptions in French — contemporary practice in the case of knights at that time.

From **Stokenchurch** village centre, take the lane opposite the King's Arms, down Coopers Court Road, by the side of the Fleur de Lis, and under the motorway by a concrete tunnel. Beyond the motorway turn right at once, cross the stile to the left of the farm gate, cross the field to the next stile near the farm and turn left alongside a hedgerow, with the hedge on your right. When the path runs down to a wood, cross a gate and continue down through a stile and keep on up with the hedge still on your right, to clear a double bar stile and so forward to reach farm cottages at a farm track. You will find a stile near the gate opposite — go over it and across grass to another stile which stands at a wood.

The path goes directly ahead under the trees, always running within sight of the wood's edge (right). There are white waymark arrows at intervals to help you. On reaching a lane, the way is leftward for half a mile to **Ibstone Common,** but you can easily walk inside the wood, using the road as a guide.

IBSTONE COMMON, where the two walk circuits join, has a string of cottages that line the road, while the open grassland gives a hint of the scenery to be enjoyed.

(1) From the Fox public house opposite the start of the open space, go half-left towards the far side by a path that follows the boundary hedgeline on to a stony track. Here, on the other side of the common, you take a clear green track, directly opposite, that runs through bushes and soon past a cottage or two to a metalled lane, where you turn right. From a height of about 700 feet at the common, the lane falls gently past several large houses and loses its surface at a wood. For a little while it continues as a rutty track with a clear path, which you should join, just left of it; then the path drops between a narrow band of trees more steeply downhill. There is a left turn on level ground; on turning right at a metalled road, you arrive at a lane opposite a stile.

Leave this lonely valley by a grassy way that runs upward from the stile to another stile hidden in the wood ahead — aim for the curve of the nearest part of the wood. Now comes a steep climb for 50 yards by a path starting a yard or so to the right of the stile until, just higher than a waymarked beech, the path reaches another thin path on the left. Join this path which runs over rough but level ground with the edge of the wood below. It is faint at first, but after 700 yards eases into a broader track. Keep straight on until, a long half-mile from its start, you strike a very pronounced track at right angles. By this, take the pleasant climb to the upper wood, emerging at the barns of **Turville Court.** From the field-gate on the left cross into a field and, with the house and grounds on the right, go over the centre of the grass to an iron gate beyond which the path crosses through another field. The path then skirts a wood and a clear path (waymarked on a telegraph pole) leads on down the valley where, on lower ground, it curves left to run between hedges to **Turville** village. On the way notice the windmill perched on the height across the fold — your next objective.

TURVILLE. The lovely old red-brick cottages lining the valley lane make this one of the most attractive villages in Buckinghamshire. There were two manors here, Turville Manor bought in 1753 by John Osborn, a famous eighteenth-century bookseller; and Turville Park, once owned by Lord Chancellor Lyndhurst. The church is heavily restored, but has a lot of interest. One of its most odd offerings to the wayfarer is the stone coffin cut from a single stone. It has a three-stepped cross on the lid. It was used for the body of a priest who died in the 1400s, but prying modern eyes arranged

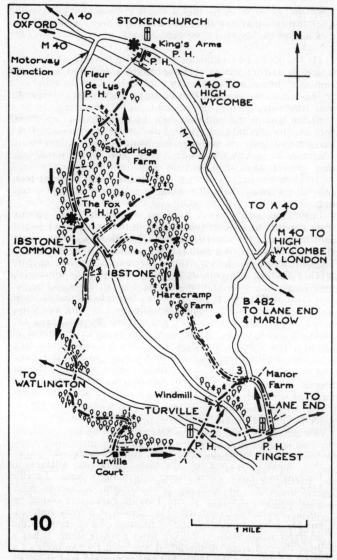

for the lid to be lifted and a mystery revealed itself. For the original occupant's remains had gone, and they found the bones of a woman, buried 'in woollen'. On one of her bones was the mark of a bullet.

A path starting between cottages at a post-box near the church runs to a stile at a steeply rising field **(2)**.

The main walk continues up the steep chalk slopes to pass the mill, which has been re-stored and re-sailed.

At the lane at the mill turn right and take a clear woodland path on the left side of the highway. Near the bottom of the wood bear right, around wire enclosing a cleared area to an avenue of beeches that in turn takes you down almost to the lane from Fingest. Do not go into the lane.

(3) Turn left by a path that runs in line with a row of trees and bushes along the valley floor, parallel with a wide grassy strip. You follow this beautiful valley now for about 1½ miles through three swing gates. Away to your right, now, are the white-painted buildings of Harecramp Farm. You pass a track on the right from the farm and later reach a crossing track by a young plantation. Take the path ahead (half-right) through the plantation.

Keeping beside the wire (left), the way bears very slightly leftwards to run near the valley floor (avoid a tempting flinty track away on your right). On reaching a stony crossing track, keep your direction through young firs and carry on, still pressing ahead along the valley by a deeply rutted track. Later the path curves slightly to the left and soon afterwards reaches a waymarked field-gate on the left. You should cross this gate and bear left, following a track between young firs to take the second 'turning' on the right so that you walk uphill between the trees to a wider space near gates. From here, follow the footpath directly on, over rising ground, that runs beside a field hedge bordered with wire. At the top the path widens and runs out to a lane, where you turn right, passing a phone-box and village notice-board to **Ibstone Common** again (1).

You can, of course, return to Stokenchurch by the woodland way you used earlier, or try the rougher footpath starting from the gravel track by Three Ways, 200 yards beyond the phone-box, on the right. This track soon falls over a field to a hedge gap, passing a farm on the right, where you reach another cleared wood — only a copse at the foot of the field below remains. Pause a moment; the next objective is the red roofs of Studdridge Farm which can be glimpsed half-left on the distant hill. The path has gone, and the easiest way is to keep near the right of the felled area by a clear farm track which passes the copse on the left on its way to lower ground. Then go leftwards, over grass and up along the right side of the field. At the top cross over into the field above, and again follow a left-hand hedge to an iron field-gate which leads to the farm. Cross a stile by the barn, along the drive through the farm, and after 100 yards swing off right to pass two tree groups (marking ponds) just on your left. Keep straight on now, parallel with the drive to the far side of the field and turn right to the bar stile at the corner. You are now on your outward route, which you follow ahead into **Stokenchurch** again.

Detour through Fingest

Follow the instructions for the main walk to the end of the paragraph marked (2). Now turn right at the crossing path and follow it to a line of trees. Keep them on your right to a lane and continue by the path opposite to Fingest church. Take the lane out of Fingest that passes Manor Farm, and rejoin the main walk at the paragraph marked (3).

Getting there

Stokenchurch: Green Line/Oxford South Midland coach 290; London (Victoria)-Uxbridge-High Wycombe-Stokenchurch-Oxford.

Bee Line bus 338 from High Wycombe.

Car parking: off the main street at Stokenchurch; also at and near Ibstone Common.

Index of Places